Visible Voices

C000047953

Nicolas Barker grew up in Cambridge, surrounded by books. The University Library taught him about their history, and the University Press taught him how to print them. He started his own press aged fourteen, but after graduating from Oxford in 1957 went into publishing, working for Rupert Hart-Davis, Macmillan's, and the Oxford University Press. He also wrote for the *TLS* and *The Book Collector*, of which he became editor in 1965. In 1976 he became first Head of Conservation of the new British Library, retiring in 1992. Since then he has been Libraries Adviser to the National Trust, and consultant to the House of Commons, the Rosenbach, Pierpont Morgan and many other libraries. He was Visiting Professor at University of California between 1986 and '87, and was elected Fellow of the British Academy in 1998. He has written or edited over thirty books, most recently *The Roxburghe Club: A Bicentenary History* (2012).

Nicolas Barker

Visible Voices

Translating Verse into Script & Print
3000 BC–AD 2000

CARCANET

First published in Great Britain in 2016 by
Carcanet Press Limited
Alliance House
Cross Street
Manchester
M2 7AQ

www.carcanet.co.uk
We welcome your comments on our publications: info@carcanet.co.uk

A CIP catalogue record for this book is available from the British Library

ISBN 978 1 84777 212 1

The publisher acknowledges financial assistance from Arts Council England

Designed and typeset by XL Publishing Services, Exmouth
Printed and bound in England by SRP Ltd, Exeter

Contents

Preface

That poetry is a memorial device, its purpose to remind audience or reader, was a fact embedded in my conscience from very early on. My parents belonged to a generation that knew a great deal of poetry by heart, learned willingly or accidentally, and often quoted it. Lord Wavell's *Other Men's Flowers* (1944) taught me how much poetry one mind, if a great one, could absorb, and also the importance of reciting it. It was not until 1950 that the task of setting in type the poems of Richard Corbet awoke me to the visual dimension of poetry, another discipline, like that of recitation. Then there was the third dimension, format. What could not be carried in the mind could still be held in the hand. C. H. Wilkinson's anthology *Diversions* (1940), made to fit in an ammunition pouch, kept poetry within reach during national service, to be recalled in need. Apprenticeship to Stanley Morison, and the task of completing his last book, *Politics and Script* (1972), made me aware of the span, in time, substance and shape, of the forms of letters and the documents that they made up. This, as far as I can remember, is where the exploration that has led to this book began.

What gave it a new sense of direction came at the end of the last millennium in the simultaneous invitation to give two series of lectures, the Panizzi lectures at the British Library and the Rosenbach lectures at the University of Pennsylvania. I had already seen, if not very clearly, that the change in all previous methods of communication brought about by the invention of printing was a watershed that could not but change even a habit of communicating so old and complicated as poetry. Besides this was another watershed, longer and more diverse, between verse as spoken or sung and verse written down. Just as reading once involved speaking the text that you saw, whether cut on stone or written on a potsherd or papyrus roll, so poems grew in the mind of the poet, to be delivered to an audience. What was spoken could be dictated to another person who could write it down, but it was already a finished form, a lyric, a stanza, sonnet or any one of the many different forms appropriate to the kind of verse that a poet undertook. But at some point habit changed; something to write on and a pen were in the poet's hand as words assembled themselves in his mind, arranged now in lines, not just determined by metre or rhyme or stress, but fitted on a piece of paper. Somewhere in these evolutionary patterns was a dividing line, that would enable me to assemble the evidence and allocate it between the two series of lectures.

Collecting the evidence was a familiar task, familiar from watching and listening to Stanley Morison and his old friend Elias Avery Lowe discussing the earliest Greek and Latin letterforms and the texts in which they were found. This task had been trans-formed during their long lives by the increasing availability of facsimiles. Exchanging photographs, annotated with significant details, was essential to their work; understanding the evolution of scripts came by this process of comparison. You had to see the real originals as well to understand the process, but photographic facsimiles were a convenient shorthand with which to convey the crucial details of script or text. The same process, I thought, could be applied to the evolution of a particular kind of text, poetry, over a longer period than Morison had studied, taking in the earlier writing in the Nilotic and Mesopotamian language systems, out of which the Graeco-Latin system had grown. I did not dare pursue it to the vast other stretches of the world's language systems, if only because I lacked the ability to comprehend them. If there were patterns of influence, signs of interaction, it would require greater knowledge and a more synthetic vision than I possessed. Coming to terms with the two linguistic systems that preceded and influenced the familiar Graeco-Latin would stretch what resources I already had.

This kind of generalising work attracts the cautious interest of specialists. I remembered when David Diringer came to Cambridge to discuss what became *The Alphabet*, a vast work of synthesis, with Sir Ellis Minns. Minns, whose linguistic reach was remarkable, warned Diringer that what he proposed to do would take him out of 'safe' waters into a sea with no chart to guide him. He would be mocked, as other discoverers had been before him. But what he would find would be its own reward. I hoped that the voyage ahead of me would be rewarded too. I was fortu-nate to find two colleagues in the British Museum (colleagues, because we shared the same building then) who were willing to help me reach back to the beginnings of recorded poetry. I found them ready to accept the notion forming in my mind, that after its first memorial beginning poetry had been influenced by the physical forms into which it was translated, a substrate (stone, clay tablet or papyrus) and the tools (chisel or pen) which inscribed them. Richard Parkinson, then in the museum's Department of Ancient Egypt and Sudan, and Christopher Walker in its Middle East Department, were kind enough to take my hesitant enquiries seriously, to find examples that seemed to fit my hypothesis, and to provide the necessary photographs.

Collecting more of these became an inseparable part of my

quest. Morison had long kept his copies of Johann Lietzmann's *Tabulae in usum scholarum* series (1910–18), which escaped the conflagration of his books and papers in 1941; I had inherited his set of Lowe's *Codices Latini Antiquiores* (1934–72), with its full range of facsimiles of the earliest Latin texts. As the quest moved into the middle ages, it became increasingly involved in other marks besides letterforms, the points and other symbols that punctuated texts to improve the reader's comprehension, and to ease recitation. I was to find the ideal guide to this in Malcolm Parkes's *Pause and Effect* (1992), which opened new insights into the visual apparatus of the transmission of poetic texts. Among my colleagues at the British Library, Scot McKendrick, now Head of Western Heritage Collections, took an unflagging interest in a field of research that now took in all the different aspects of poetic texts in a growing number of European languages. Thanks to the generosity of the Panizzi Foundation, I was able to translate this into a series of photographs that accompanied a growing descriptive text. Stephen Parkin, Curator of the Italian Printed Collections, facilitated this increasingly important part of my subject.

As the magic of the poet's own hand began to spread over a landscape of texts preserved in otherwise secondary copies, I came to rely more on the work of earlier friends, Peter Croft and Philip Gaskell. Croft's *Autograph Poetry in the English Language: Facsimiles of Original Manuscripts from the Fourteenth to the Twentieth Century* (1972) provided a series of reproductions of rare quality (essential to capture the marks made by pens often too slow to keep up with the writer's transient thoughts), and with them transcripts and commentary that raised both to a new level of sensitivity. The same could be said of Gaskell's *From Writer to Reader: Studies in Editorial Method* (1978), which followed the author's manuscript through successive manuscript forms into printer's type, corrected proofs, print, revision and final text in eleven different cases from Sir John Harington's *Orlando Furioso* to Sir Tom Stoppard's *Travesties*. (The continuing significance of punctuation was subtly revealed in John Lennard's *But I Digress: The Exploitation of Parentheses in English Printed Verse* (1991).)

That part of the quest dealt with in the Panizzi lectures in 2001 was advertised under the title '"Things not reveal'd": the mutual impact of idea and form in the transmission of verse 2000 BC – AD 1500', the quotation from Milton reflecting my growing belief that there was in all the examples I had pursued something not obvious in the congruence of idea and form. Thanks to a long consultancy with the Rosenbach Museum and Library at Philadelphia I was able to examine the continuity of this theme directly in the case of Burns and Keats, and the Rosenbach Lecture series at the University of Pennsylvania provided the opportunity to bring it to a conclusion, if not an end, in 2002. I owe a particular debt to Derick Dreher and Elizabeth Fuller at the Rosenbach Museum and Library, and Peter Stallybrass at the University of Pennsylvania, for their help and practical support. As visual imagery became an increasingly important element in the chase, I was glad to find in Graham Robb's *Unlocking Mallarmé* (1996) 'a guided tour' through 'Un Coup de Dés'. I was also lucky to have the timely help of Elizabeth James, Senior Librarian at the National Art Library, in pursuing the concrete poetry and poets of the last century, not least in delivering my last image, downloaded from the ether, 'Mesostics for Dick Higgins', a mobile acrostic moving at ten seconds per line by mIEKAL aND. To all these, to those who have supplied images and permission to reproduce them, in particular the Curators of the Bodleian Library, Oxford, the Syndics of Cambridge University Library, the Master and Fellows of Trinity College and Corpus Christi College, Cambridge, and to those whose permission I have through ignorance been obliged to take for granted, I am grateful for their generosity. My greatest debt is to the London Library and its staff, without which the whole venture would have been impossible.

The results of these ensuing 'Notes of a Twelve Years' Voyage of Discovery', to paraphrase James Henry, might never have gone beyond the two sympathetic audiences in London and Philadelphia but for what I believe to be the perceptive faith of Michael Schmidt of Carcanet Press. He saw what I had been trying to do, and made 'a leap into the dark' by offering to publish it. By now technology had moved on, and although my text (or thesis) had not much changed, other than by correction of its more obvious errors, my photographs, obtained by the generosity of the Panizzi Foundation, lent or given by friends (notably Dr Ian Doyle), or taken by myself, were all on 35mm film. They had now to be translated into digital images. For this, and many other beneficial changes, I am indebted to John Hodgson at the John Rylands Library and Fergus Wilde at Chetham's Hospital and Library, both in Manchester. That this in turn has become a book is due to the infinite care of its editors, Helen Tookey and Luke Allan, to whom its handsome appearance is also due. To them, to all those mentioned above, to the many others who have helped along the way, I offer profound thanks.

Prologue: To Be Read Aloud

The words and lines that make up verse are now a thing we just see; no more we think to use our ears to sense what else there must be hid in the bare words that look so terse but sound in the mind. The thrust we feel now may go back to times when first man tried to keep and trust the peremptory power of words to express ideas and facts and notions about the world, to try and guess the source of life, the oceans and mountains and trees whose large excess stirred religious emotions, while human deeds could stir no less, like the wars of the Greeks and Trojans. The need to pray or praise, as time went on (the two were not then distinct), found words no less sublime, that could not be forgotten: the bards who would Parnassus climb made sure that they were not, when alliteration, metre, rhyme, came to their aid. But what then?

What indeed, you may well say. Every word you have spoken so far has employed all three of those devices, although I have done my best to conceal it: alliteration, several times, the metre and rhyme of that most familiar of ballad stanzas, 8.7.8.7.8.7. — We could have sung it together to the tune of 'The Vicar of Bray'. I don't expect you to remember what you have just recited, but I will, because I had to fit what I wanted you to say to the set of rules that helped me memorise the words. For both of us, it is a reminder of the memorial function of verse. The need to remember words and the aural and oral tricks — *now there's another, assonance, that plays its own tricks: how do you know which I meant first, your hearing or my speech? — the tricks* by which remembering was achieved, both are a reminder that memory itself was the primal need that verse came to answer.

1
Before the Alphabet

The art of remembering words has a history far longer than the history of writing, a history paradoxically forgotten, since the whole aim of writing was to supplement, and thus supersede, memory. But if the verbal devices by which we recognise verse were originally memorial in function, they came to have their own discipline: matter followed form, as well as dictating it. Nor was verse the sole mnemonic system for recording words: rhetoric and theology had different memorial needs, and developed different ways of meeting them. The orator had not only to remember the matter of his discourse, but also to set it out according to established rules.[1] The preacher had similar rules for engaging his audience, which, like the orator's, measured his success by the degree to which he kept to them. The methods that both developed were often analogous to those of verse, and not infrequently overlapped each other. But verse had separated itself from all forms of prose long before the first preserved records of either came into existence, records preserved by means of writing.

That is not to say that these genres are always easy to tell apart, even in the written forms in which they have (for the most part) come down to us. The matter is complicated by the wide gaps in time that may separate the time of composition from the time of record, and the equally wide gaps that separate the emergence of verse (let alone its record) in different parts of the world. Thus,

It is possible to think of the poets of Sigurd and Brynhild as holding among the Northern nations of the tenth or eleventh century the place that is held in every generation by some set of authors who, for the time, are at the head of intellectual or literary adventure, who hold authority, from Odin or the Muses, to teach their contemporaries one particular kind of song, till the time comes when their vogue is exhausted, and they are succeeded by other masters and other schools. This commission has been held by various kinds of author since the beginning of history, and manifold are the lessons that have been recommended to the world by their authority; now epic, now courtly and idealistic lyric, romantic drama, pedantic tragedy, funeral orations, analytical novels. They are not all amusing, and not all their prices are more than the rate of an old song. But they all have a value as trophies, as monuments of what was most important in their time, of the things in which the generations, wise and foolish, have put their trust and their whole soul.[2]

Those words aptly summarise not only the vast abysses of time and place that separate the different manifestations of verse, but also the essential unity of purpose that links bards and poets and makes them different from kings, priests and administrators, generals, merchants and accountants, and others with an interest in preserving words. Ker was thinking of the sagas, product of those independent colonists who (like the Pilgrim Fathers later) set up a new society in Iceland and deliberately cut themselves off from developments on the mainland of Europe. Those poems, relic of a heroic age, miraculously preserved in the 'Elder Edda', still survived in the Faroe ballads. This is a relatively 'late' example of survival, though not so late as the lays of the Kuba *muyum*, the Congolese bards whose task was to memorise and recite the genealogies of their kings; their span and veracity can be tested by the interpolation of eclipses and other natural phenomena, and have only recently been recorded.[3] But if oral transmission and the sound of words is a far older and far more central feature of the development and history of verse than what the eye sees in its translation into visual form, it is the latter, not the former, that has secured its survival.

Traduttore, traditore: every translation is a betrayal. Reading verse, as opposed to speaking or listening to it, loses something. The mind's ear is not so agile as the mind's eye. Subtleties of assonance are less easily appreciated on the page than the beginnings and ends of lines, or rhyme-words, similarly (or, as striking, dissimilarly) spelt. Yet the movement of the poet's eye, from line to line, column to column, or even across the page, with the reader in pursuit, has its own poetry. If sound is the ultimate criterion of verse, the visible pattern that it makes cannot be ignored. The loss and gain in translation from spoken to written verse is itself but a reflection of the more complex and longer process of transition involved in the need to create a visible record of speech. *Nescit vox missa reverti*: if a word once spoken cannot come back, it may escape altogether. So the slow movement from pictogram to phonetic symbol to script is itself a self-referential process of translation; the image of the student devising his own shorthand in a desperate attempt to keep up with the lecturer's words while struggling simultaneously to comprehend them is not a remote analogy. Nor is it just a question of 'keeping up' with the speed of speech. The idea in the mind of the poet is itself imperfectly captured in words, as authorial change, in draft, fair copy, proof, print, and any subsequent manifestation, all too often shows. An idea, an image, here may have started somewhere else, beyond the author's control if not ken; it may end ages later, in the hands of an editor, translator, reader, when it may take on quite different adumbrations and resonances.

When we say that reading verse loses something, we now think of reading as to one's self, silently. But reading, etymologically, implies reading aloud, and it is important to remember not only that texts were composed and then written down to be read aloud for far longer than those destined for silent reading, but also that other texts had as long a life or longer before any means of recording them existed at all. What we now have to do is to go backwards: back, that is, not only towards the unretrievable notion first expressed in words that imperfectly rendered it even then, before they achieved a greater durability and a changed form in writing, but also to the roots of that form, the sources of the graphic expression that is all we have of the earliest surviving verse.

This second quest is yet further complicated by the fact that these roots have themselves been recovered in only recent time, and, confusingly, in reverse chronological order. The oldest languages are those we have most recently learned to read. Thanks to the Rosetta Stone in Egypt, Young and Champollion, and later Lepsius, worked back through Greek and Coptic to demotic and hieroglyph. These semantic systems (and the intervening hieratic script) paralleled but did not wholly correspond with the linguistic changes from Old to Middle (or classical) Egyptian, between 3300 and 1300 BC, and from Late Egyptian to demotic and Coptic, up to the fifteenth century AD. Similarly, when it came to cuneiform, Niebuhr, Grotefend and Rawlinson, who discovered the trilingual inscription at Behistun, moved from the alphabetic old Persian, to the syllabic Elamite, back to the more ideographic 'third script', then called 'Assyrian'. This proved to be the complex vehicle of two languages, Akkadian and the earlier Sumerian, finally distinguished by Thureau-Dangin. The earliest pictograms of Uruk *c.* 3000 BC (still not wholly decipherable 'shorthand' records of transactions) were expanded phonetically to absorb two language systems, the agglutinative Sumerian and the inflected Semitic Akkadian that superseded but did not abolish the older tongue. As systematised in the scribal schools and copying centres of Assyria and Babylon, cuneiform script could be used to represent both languages, which were structurally and aurally quite different. This gave it a flexibility that enabled it to become the vehicle of other languages – Elamite, Hurrian, Hittite, and their descendants.

It is thus only by going back to their roots that it has become possible to trace how words and scripts and texts developed. None of these languages existed as a spoken tongue in modern times (except, up to the fifteenth century, liturgical Coptic), and the actual sounds of consonants and phonemes have had to be derived from their descendants. The languages of Egypt and Mesopotamia exist only in written form, which gives that form a special significance as the sole vehicle of the texts it conveys. The form is the cause of their preservation. Furthermore, words, in prose or verse, are only part of all that is signified by a monument. The making of a monument conveys a complex of messages, in which its dimensions, its shape and its design all participate. The words on it are only another part, perhaps only a footnote to the message as a whole. Material too has a part, whether planned or not by its creator. Papyrus rolls or clay tablets exercise their own formal influence on the messages that they preserve. This can make it both easier and harder to determine whether these are in prose or verse. Is an invocation or prayer, a spell or incantation, a poem?

In the case of the texts carved on the walls of the sarcophagus chamber and adjoining rooms of the Pyramid of Unas, the last Fifth Dynasty King (d. *c.* 2300 BC), at Saqqara, there is little doubt:

Incantation texts, Pyramid of Unas, *c.* 2300BC; British Museum, EA 10127.

All Pyramid Texts are composed in the 'orational style', a recitative that depends for its effects on a strong regular rhythm. Here and there, when suffused with feeling and imagination,

the incantations attain the heightened intensity which is the universal hall-mark of poetry.[4]

The texts represent the journey of the dead king to become one with the gods: his awakening in the tomb, ritual cleansing, journey through the stars to the eastern sky and union with Re, the sun-god. Set out in vertical hieroglyphic lines, separated by parallel rules, they cover the walls of the entrance chamber, and can be seen above and to left and right of the doorway of the tomb itself. Many similar inscriptions in symmetrically patterned phrases, some autobiographical, are carved on the pyramids of the 'street of tombs' at Saqqara.

The Sixth Dynasty inscription on the tomb of Sheshi, also at Saqqara, is an epitaph in the form of an autobiography, again composed in symmetrically patterned phrases. The text is set out in three columns and repeated on each side of the false-door of the tomb, with the name of the deceased at the foot, above his portrait in relief. These elements are all part of the decoration of the tomb, and the epitaphic autobiography is an expansion of the name and title of the occupant, a caption (so to speak) of the image.

Prayer to Osiris, Stele of Intef, *c.* 1900BC; British Museum, EA 581.

The 'Instruction of Ptahhotep' is an example of another popular genre of Old Kingdom texts, the 'Instruction in Wisdom', of which the biblical Book of Proverbs is a familiar example, prescribing justice and moderation. Although Ptahhotep himself was apparently a historical figure, vizier to King Isesi in the Fifth Dynasty, his 'Instruction' only exists in the form of papyri of the Middle Kingdom, and the text is probably no older. If there was an Old Kingdom original, it must have been substantially rewritten and enlarged. Most Egyptologists now agree that it is a historical fiction, probably composed at the beginning of the Twelfth Dynasty (*c.* 1990 BC).[5] With Egyptian, as (*ceteris paribus*) with Greek literature, the 'earliest' texts prove to be a literary back-projection of later years.

The stele of Intef, son of Sent, from Abydos (*c.* 1900 BC?) begins with an invocation addressed to Osiris, its seven horizontal lines beside the figure of Intef. This is followed by the 'epitaph', which is written underneath the invocation in vertical lines. It is written in the same autobiographic style as that of Sheshi, set out in two registers, one above the other, each with ten columns, each column beginning with an assertion 'I am…', followed by a statement of one of Intef's virtues, which correspond with those expounded in the maxims of Ptahhotep.

Stone is indestructible, and inscriptions on it permanent. Other forces may belie their words, as Shelley knew ('Look on my works…'), but they have another disadvantage for both writer and reader: they are also immobile. Texts written on other, lighter materials are portable, more obedient to the reader's needs, and may, after all, survive the risks of time. The papyrus reed grows and dies like any other vegetable, but its fibres, pounded flat, formed sheets that could be written on and pasted together in rolls. These were the main vehicle for preserving any text, whether verse or business accounts. If one such use became obsolete, the reverse could be used for another. Finally discarded, they could be recycled; even if thrown away, many survived burial in the warm dry sands of Egypt.

So far the texts considered have all been monumental in purpose and physical form. If the 'Instruction of Ptahhotep' had a real original, it is lost. What we now read is not merely historical fiction, but in a different medium. The creation of both text and medium is due to another basic human need, education. A single group of papyri now at Berlin, in hieratic script set out in vertical columns, reflect not merely scholastic need but a considerable advance in textual sophistication. The most famous, 'The Tale of Sinuhe', may have been composed only a little after the death of the official Intef about 1800 BC, but the adventures of Sinuhe,

'The Tale of Sinuhe',
c. 1800BC, papyrus roll;
Berlin, Staatsbibliothek,
P.Berlin 3022.

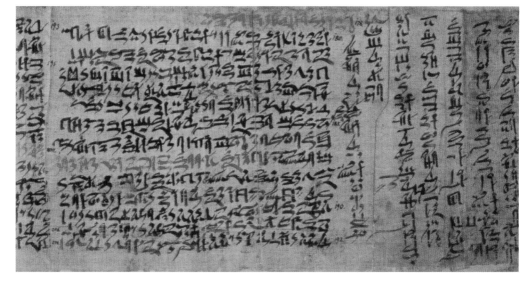

like him a court servant, seem aeons away in terms of imaginative scope, style and matter. Although his account begins in the same strain of autobiographical epitaph, the narrative of Sinuhe's panic in the aftermath of the (implied) assassination of his master, Amenemhat I, his flight beyond the northern confines of the Kingdom, how he prospered there, but eventually returned to the court and favour of Senwosret I, is as exciting as any ballad. The text, to us so vivid, was popular for educational use, and its physical form changed in time in interesting ways. The papyrus texts are written continuously in columns with no stichic arrangement (that is, by verse-lines) or indentation. Some of them use rubrics to introduce the start of stanzas, but do so only sporadically, and without verse-points. But the text also survives in a Ramesside copy, an ostrakon, a fragment of pottery; here the lines are set out horizontally, right to left, with inserted punctuation in red, a device for improving delivery when read aloud.

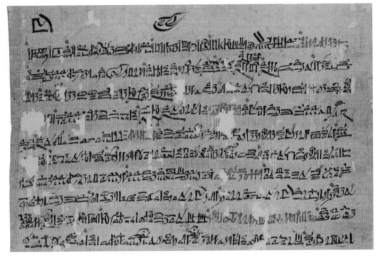

'Teaching of Amenemhat', *c.* 1220–1200BC, papyrus roll; British Museum, EA 10182 (P.Sallier II.1).

Like 'The Tale of Sinuhe', 'The Teaching of Amenemhat I' presupposes the King's death, and the advice it gives to his son, Senwosret I, is not just a historical reconstruction, but a powerful rhetorical statement for contemporary application.[6] In cultural terms, it is like the speeches in Shakespeare: the words of Caesar, Macbeth or Richard II are his; the audience, his Elizabethan contemporaries, were less interested in the historical veracity of the text than its message for them. The composition, according to surviving texts, was the work of the scribe Khety. The same writer was also held responsible for the 'Satire of the Trades', an 'Instruction' text of a humbler kind, the more interesting for the light that it throws on the scribe's profession. Here, as in Ecclesiasticus 38.24–30, the lasting work of the scribe is contrasted with the vain labour of all the other craftsmen; evidently, the author of Ecclesiasticus was familiar with this text.[7]

The scribe of this papyrus, one of the first to be brought back from Egypt and seen by Champollion in 1830, signs his name 'Inena' on one of the other texts in the roll, towards the end of the thirteenth century. He wrote a fine hieratic script, although not without fault, since the text is corrected in line 2: 'may you govern' appears in superscript against the more conventional 'may you rule'; while the signs for a pair of arms holding a shield and for a crocodile were rendered imperfectly in lines 8 and 2, and appear in correct and enlarged form at the top. It is one of a number of such manuscripts, copied by advanced apprentices under the direction of a master-scribe, to whom the apprentices dedicate them. Note again the rubricated opening phrases of each stanza (the text runs on otherwise), and also the red dot (equivalent to the 'punctus elevatus' of later times) that indicates the ends of lines (the minute numbers are Champollion's).

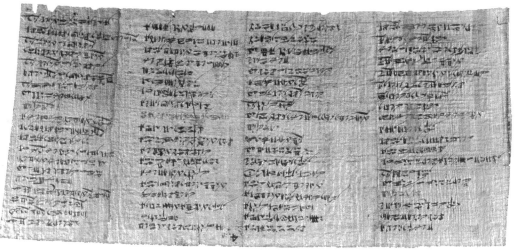

'The Teaching of Amenemope', *c.* 1200BC, papyrus roll; British Museum, EA 10474.

Perhaps the longest continuous poem to survive from ancient Egyptian literature, certainly the longest didactic text, is the 'Instruction of Amenemope', which dates from the Ramesside period.[8] The text consists of a series of injunctions, set out in stichic verse and divided into thirty chapters. It is, as its prologue declares, 'The beginning of the teaching for life, the instruction for well-being'. The British Museum papyrus, which preserves the entire text, is written stichically, and the chapter divisions are marked as such. Within the chapters, the lines are linked by 'parallelism' (repetition by paraphrase, a memorial device familiar to us from the Psalms) into groups of two, three or four lines. Here again, the biblical echo is no accident. The 'Instruction' is coeval with the enforced stay of the Children of Israel in Egypt, and the Book of Proverbs is full of echoes of it, notably in chapters 22–23. 'Have I not written for you thirty sayings of admonition and knowledge?' (22.20) may be a direct reference to Amenemope.

The BM papyrus concludes with a scribal colophon, recording its writing by 'Senu, son of the divine father Pemu'.

Another poem, preserved in a scribal exercise, reflects the same religious didacticism. If sceptical of the afterlife as such, the poet sees a better hope of immortality in words that anticipate Callimachus's epitaph for Heraclitus, a thousand years later. Ironically, the copyist seems to have missed the sentence division and metrical structure; there is no red verse-pointing, although the stanzas are marked by rubrication of the first words.

> Be a scribe! Put it in your heart,
> that your name shall exist like theirs!
> The roll is more excellent than the carved stele,
> than the enclosure which is established.
> These act as chapels and pyramids
> in the heart of him who pronounces their names.
> Surely a name in mankind's mouth
> stands out in the graveyard…
> These sages, who foretold what comes –
> what came from their mouths happened –
> one benefits from the lines
> written in their books.
> To them the offspring of others are given,
> to be heirs as if their own children.
> They hid from the masses their magic,
> which is read from their Teachings.
> Departing life has made their names forgotten;
> it is writings that make them remembered.[9]

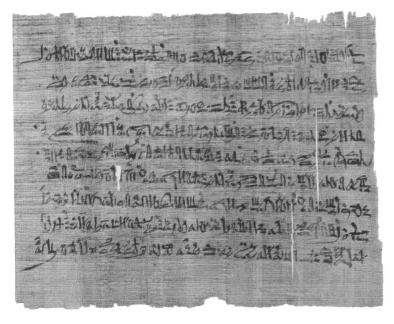

Love Songs Cycle, *c.* 1200BC, papyrus roll; Dublin, Chester Beatty Library, P. Chester Beatty I.

The fine Ramesside Papyrus Chester Beatty I contains a cycle of love poems, of considerable sophistication in terms of content, and also in the quite complex organisation of the sequence.[10] Each of the seven stanzas has a numbered heading, the number repeated or implied by the use of a homophonic word in the first and last line (also homotypic, since *sen* means 'brother' but also stands for the figure '2'). The lines themselves are divided into distichs or quatrains, with verse-points. These are not all correctly placed, as if the scribe had not fully understood the text. These artifices, however, even the play of words, are all more scribal than authorial – unlike the Greek acrostic poems that Alexandrian poets and their audience enjoyed.

The informality of these last texts strikes us as astonishingly modern, closer, at least, to what we expect of poetry. But this is fortuitous, or rather the result of the eternal sameness of the subject. It would be more reasonable to seize on the resemblances between the 'Tale of Sinuhe' and the *Odyssey*. What is more startling is the realisation that most of these texts were composed and some written before the nucleus of the *Iliad* came into existence, even if there is as great a distance, in some cases, between date of composition and date of earliest surviving text. There is, obviously, a distance between the stele and the roll, between verse as monument and verse as aide-memoire or even school-exercise, a distance often in time as well as space. But such distances are also a reminder that verse has another dimension, in performance. Even if writing is all we have with which to reconstruct that other dimension, it must remind us, forcibly, that writing is but a memento of an event in which verse was only a part. Yet, if not forgetting performance, we must remember that all this, the ceremony with words spoken or chanted, the inscription on the unmoving stone, the copy on papyrus that might divulgate it, was part of a memorial process, which was itself the life-blood of society and the mainstay of the cosmic order. This was as true on the Tigris and Euphrates as on the Nile.

If there are similarities between the development of Akkadian and Egyptian script and texts, in the demand for memorial record, in diglossia (the simultaneous use of two languages),[11] in the movement from pictogram to phonetic system, in the use of 'classifiers' and 'determinants' to avoid ambiguity, and in its maintenance by a 'scholarly' class, there are also considerable differences. Egypt, despite its cultural complexity, was essentially a unitary society, while the nascent Mesopotamian cities of Assyria and Babylonia were more like the Greek city-states that came later, with the same urgent need for commerce and its record, the same free association of temporal and spiritual power, tyrant and temple. The two languages of Egypt evolved over time, classical and demotic diverging in ways different from the scripts by which they were conveyed. Sumerian and Akkadian had different roots before there was any script to record either; the evolution of cuneiform was an exercise in compromise, compromise that had far-reaching consequences, of which the preservation of Sumerian, isolated like Latin as a 'classical' tongue, was one.

The radical difference between the native speech of Uruk and Ur, Nippur and Lagash, and the incoming Semitic Akkadian, which coincided with the rise of Sargon as overlord of the southern cities (2335–2279 BC), forced and accelerated the movement from pictogram to phonetic rendering. In this, consonantal groups dominated, vowel sounds being assumed, hence the need for 'classifiers'. The emphasis on the names of things, persons and gods as part of their essence, which is so marked a feature of Akkadian texts, may be another aspect of this syncretic impulse.

The Sumerian goddess Inanna, the Akkadian Ishtar, was the goddess of love and war, equated with the planet Venus; her descent into the underworld was a prominent part of Babylonian mythology. The 'Hymn to Ishtar' consists of 14 stanzas, concluding with a prayer that the goddess will give long life to Ammiditana, King of Babylon (*c.* 1683–1647 BC), which provides a date for the composition of the hymn.[12] The opening stanzas are divided into two parts, the second repeating the first, sometimes in the same words, a form of parallelism familiar from the Psalms. Sung in Sumerian (by now a liturgical language, as Latin and Coptic became after they had ceased to be the vehicle of everyday speech), this structure may indicate that it was rendered antiphonally, that is, by two alternating choirs.[13] The text is set out in alternate lines, the original Sumerian and the Akkadian translation, with the final colophon between parallel lines at the end.

At the other end of the scale of literary texts is a farcical dialogue between an elegant and demanding fop and his laundryman, the young man giving endless directions till the laundryman tells him to mind his own business ('*If you know so much about it, why don't you do it yourself?*'). The whole poem is in direct speech, although the change of speakers is not marked, and extends over two tablets. Each tenth line is numbered. As is customary in Old Babylonian, the signs are hung from lines that were not ruled in advance, but written freehand; inevitably, the written area tends to tilt upwards. Both tablets are in unusually good condition, the first all but undamaged; the grey colour of the clay is an indication of their Babylonian source.[14]

After Layard's discovery of Nineveh, the event in the rediscovery of the Mesopotamian past that most caught public

Epic of Gilgamesh, clay
tablet from Ashurbanipal's
Palace, *c.* 685–627BC;
British Museum, K3375.

Poem of the Righteous
Sufferer, clay tablet from
Ashurbanipal's Palace,
c. 685–627BC; British
Museum K3972/8396.

imagination was George Smith's revelation, on 3 December 1872, of a Flood narrative too close to Genesis to be accidental. 'Atrahasis' survives in four versions, of which the Old Babylonian or classical text originally consisted of 1245 lines of verse on three tablets, of which about sixty per cent survives, in whole or in part. One fragment contains the beginning of the story, when the gods plan the flood to extinguish mankind; Enki/Ea, father of Marduk, the deity of Babylon, warns Atrahasis, who prepares a boat to escape in. It bears a colophon at the foot of the reverse of the tablet recording that it was written in the twelfth year of Ammisaduqa, King of Babylon (1635 BC).[15]

The 'Epic of Gilgamesh' was as striking a discovery to a generation newly attuned to Beowulf and the Nibelungenlied.[16] The adventures of Gilgamesh and Enkidu, and Gilgamesh's fruitless journey in search of eternal life, had the same timeless quality. Although fragments of one or more Old Babylonian versions exist, the Ninevite version from Ashurbanipal's palace is the fullest (about three quarters complete). Like other texts from the palace, it is carefully finished, its two columns with the lines stretched to fill the space of the obverse, without turning over on to the edges, as did tablets from less prestigious collections.

Descent of Ishtar, clay tablet from Ashurbanipal's Palace, *c.* 685–627BC; British Museum, K162.

The remarkable text known as the 'Poem of the Righteous Sufferer'[17] is another biblical analogue, in this case with the Book of Job. Apparently datable to the thirteenth century BC, it is a text of great virtuosity, employing rare words, paronomasia by sound and sign, alliteration, rhyme, intricate parallelism, as well as overarching thematic divisions, for example when mood and metaphor move from dark to light. The text was very popular, and copies from different places are known, as well as an old commentary. Two fragments of Tablet 2 are from an Assyrian version, with the colophon indicating that it was made for the library of Ashurbanipal. The conspicuous holes are a relic of the firing-process; the line-extensions are not so visible in this as they are in the second.

Ishtar's continuing hold on her worshippers is shown by later manifestations of it. The only complete text of the 'Great Prayer to Ishtar', known from a Hittite text that dates back to the later second millennium BC, was written *c.* 600 BC.[18] It was incised with great skill by a professional scribe, who wrote it 'for his livelihood' to be placed in the Temple of Marduk Esagila at Babylon and recorded that it was 'copied from a tablet at Borsippa [just south of Babylon] by Nergal-balassu-Iqbi'. Rather than strain the script to fill the line, he left blanks. The 'Descent of Ishtar' to the Underworld is a vivid narrative, set out here in a Neo-Assyrian tablet (*c.* 650 BC) in two narrow columns with conspicuous line-ruling, with signs stretched, but not to fill the lines.[19]

Akkadian writers of this period, rather like those who, a thousand years later, frequented the library at Alexandria, rejoiced in word-play of all sorts. The 'Prayer to Nabu'[20] is a compound acrostic. The text, again with biblical overtones of 'He hath put down the mighty from their seat, and hath exalted the humble and meek. He hath filled the hungry with good things and the rich he hath sent empty away', is an acrostic of four lines, each beginning with the same syllable, the quatrains ruled off from each other horizontally. The syllables of each would have spelt out a message, but as the tablet is barely a third complete, it remains indecipherable. The 'Babylonian Theodicy'[21] is a debate on divine justice in dialogue form between two friends, the younger complaining of the unfairness of the world, the older and wiser counselling acceptance of what cannot be fully understood. The tablet is split into four columns vertically, each corresponding to a syllable or group of syllables. Anyone familiar with the scansion scheme of, say, elegiac couplets will instantly see a resemblance to the feet of hexameter or pentameter. This is not an exact parallel: Akkadian verse was rhythmic, not metrical. Here again there is an acrostic: each 18-line stanza begins with the same syllable, and the combined syllables make up the legend 'I, Siggilkinamubbib, am adorant of god and king'. The three initial syllables of the three stanzas on this tablet, 'a – nu – ku', simply mean 'I', which shows the extraordinary contrast between the spatial condensation and syllabic extent of Akkadian verse. It is most unusual, even as late as the seventh century BC, for the writers of such poetry to admit authorship, and still rarer to find the name inscribed on the tablet.

If there are constant echoes in the subjects and treatment of texts in the two great riverine cultures, it is as well to remember that in one particular where similarity might have been expected, script, there is none. The translation of speech to symbol, the base material, the instruments, all were different. But the role of the scribe in society, whether learned scholar or humble copyist, was indeed similar, as was belief in the memorial power of script.

The east wall of the pronaos of the temple of Horus at Edfu in Upper Egypt, built in the first century BC, has a frieze showing Ptolemy X offering a palette and an inkwell to Thoth, Seshat and seven falcon-headed gods, who are called 'The Utterances'; they personify the written word, and have 'caused memory to begin because they wrote'. The inscription reads:

> These mighty ones created writing in the beginning in order to establish heaven and earth in their moment … lords of the art of acting exactly, a mooring post for those who travel on mud, craftsmen of knowledge, leaders of teaching, nurses of the person who fashions perfect words, lords of the standard, rulers of accounts, whose true work is everything that ensures the well-being of the entire land; shepherds of the whole world, who steer perfectly without falling into the water, fulfilling the need of all that is and all that is not, reassuring the hearts of the gods, and taking care of the established world, its watchmen, who watch without sleeping, labouring unpaid in the fields, excellent ones who bring the rulership of the land, who reckon the confines of the four corners of the sky, who provide the offering tables of the great gods, and the fields of the officials, who guide everyone to their share, judging truthfully without the bribes that everyone else relies on in their trade. The heir speaks with his forefathers, when they have passed from the heart: a wonder of their excelling fingers, so that friends can communicate when the sea is between them, and one man can hear another without seeing him.[22]

2
The Alphabet: From East to West

The second half of the second millennium BC was a period of change and movement, political and social, in the Near East, during which the two riverine cultures were brought closer together. It began with the long reign of Thutmose III, during which Egyptian power was extended as far as northern Syria, while Mesopotamia marked time under Kassite (south-east) and Mitanni (north-west) rule. The Hittite empire expanded east and south from Anatolia, halting Rameses II at Qadesh (1293 BC), only to succumb to the 'people of the sea' from the north-west. Trade followed movement, and with trade went the need to communicate. If Akkadian became, to some extent, its lingua franca, the versatility of cuneiform made it the vehicle of other languages; other peoples, notably the Hittites, adapted it. Ugarit (Ras Shamra, on the Mediterranean coast between Aleppo and Damascus) was at the epicentre of this linguistic adaptation. There, beside classical Babylonian texts (the 'Epic of Gilgamesh' and the poem of the 'Righteous Sufferer'), have been found Ugaritic cuneiform texts, rendered by some thirty signs corresponding with consonants, a recognisable alphabet.[1] But if the alphabet thus rendered in cuneiform met the needs of Ugarit, it did not originate there.

The language used there and by other Semitic people in Syria and Palestine was 'Canaanite'. Apart from the Ugarit clay tablets, the form of letters found on Canaanite inscriptions on stone (mid–ninth century BC) is already cursive, suggesting derivation from forms earlier written, on papyrus or leather. The source came to light in Gardiner's identification of eleven short inscriptions found at the site of the Egyptian temple of the goddess Hathor at Serabit-el-Khadim on the Sinai peninsular. The signs were pictorial, like but not the same as Egyptian hieroglyphs. Egyptian, however, besides other ideographic and phonetic signs, also had signs for single consonants, univocal, unlike the multivocal Akkadian signs. These must have suggested the signs for Canaanite sounds, a bull's head for *'alef* (ox), the square box (already an Egyptian sign) for *beth* (house), a hump for *gimel* (camel); acrophonic derivation was, again, already familiar in cuneiform. There were turquoise mines at Serabit-el-Khadim, worked during the Twelfth and again from the Eighteenth to Twentieth Dynasties, and the presence of Semitic miners is recorded in Egyptian inscriptions there dating

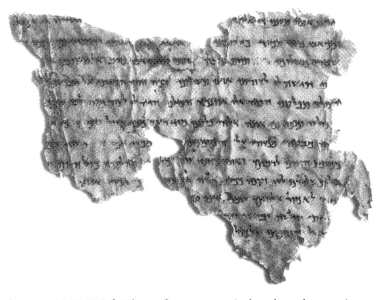

Dead Sea Psalm Scroll, Qumran, 11QPs[a], 30–50AD; A. Sanders, *The Psalm Scroll of Qumrân Cave 11* (Oxford, 1965); P.W. Flint, *The Dead Sea Psalms Scrolls* (Leiden, 1997).

from *c.* 1800 BC.[2] These facts are typical rather than unique: no doubt there were other parallel and similar processes, but if the alphabet can be said to have a beginning, it lies somewhere between Egypt and Mesopotamia, in a Canaanite need to isolate consonantal sounds and give them graphic form, adapting both established forms of script to this end. It is the height of irony that the two great systems of language and script then current should have combined to provide the means by which both were lost, until recovered in the nineteenth century AD.[3]

Accident preserved the earliest documents of the languages and script that replaced them. Old people can still remember the excitement caused by the discovery of the Dead Sea Scrolls between 1946 and 1956; their grandparents were as excited about the recovery of papyri, mostly in Greek, in Egypt. Many of the texts were ancient, and if few of the documents found were as old as their texts, they were a great deal nearer the source than anything else that had survived. For the first time, it became possible to construct a tangible line, however tenuous, back to the earliest known poetry.

Poetry in both classical Egyptian and Akkadian had regularly used pairing, both as visually presented formal structures and in composition: in stanzas arranged in distichs and quatrains (pairs of distichs), and in what Robert Lowth was the first to call 'parallelism',[4] the repetition of an expression in the first half of a verse paraphrased in the second half. The Hebrew Psalms provide a familiar example of both types. In their earliest preserved form, the fragments of some 30 distinct rolls found in caves at or near Qumran on the north-west shore of the Dead Sea, written about the turn of the era, are in a script little different in essentials from the Hebrew familiar today. It is of the kind called 'square' or 'Assyrian', derived from the Aramaic or eastern form of alphabetic Semitic script. It is only strange to our eye in lacking vowel points and cantilation (chanting) signs, still omitted in Torah rolls. The squareness of the script, hung from the ruled line, is accentuated not diminished by the one ascending letter, *lamed*. So far as can now be seen, the texts were written in columns of varying widths, about 15.5–18 cm wide and 24–27 lines deep, either on skins or papyrus. The skins are ruled individually with a blind point and sewn together with linen thread, through holes set diagonally. There are only occasional headings, and the verses (as we think of them) are not marked as such; instead, pericopes (such as the beginnings and endings of psalms, or passages designated for liturgical use) are broken off as paragraphs, and pauses marked by spaces on the line, filling it out to the end for an open pericope, shorter for a closed pericope. It is a system well adapted to a document intended for recitation or chanting. Other papyrus fragments are not the only ones to supplement this with rubrication for the opening words of the pericope, an Egyptian trait for an Egyptian substrate.[5]

This system of dividing the text for oral delivery was not new, and, although other more elaborate methods of setting out the Hebrew text were devised, the use of space to punctuate the Psalms continued in other languages, both Greek and Latin. But other means of punctuation existed, overlapping with this and each other. Few of the earliest manuscripts in either language bear witness to this, but the instructions for the division of texts for rhetorical or grammatical purposes (that is, as spoken or written), laid down by the great Roman authority on rhetoric, Quintilian, into *sententiae*, *cola*, *commata* (roughly: period, clause and phrase) or by the Greek grammarian Aristophanes of Byzantium, who introduced points, breathings and accents as a guide to pronunciation, were certainly known and sometimes applied.[6] As the surviving texts are almost all in *scriptio continua*, continuous unbroken strips of letters without word-division, the need was and is conspicuous: the fact remains that the use of punctuation in manuscripts is not found early.

The earliest substantial Greek verse manuscript to survive, the *Persae* of Timotheus (fourth century BC), is not punctuated, nor is there any division of verses or lines; only the sections of the text are marked off by starting a new line. The layout of a third-century fragment of a lyric by Archilochus suggests that the complete text was lineated.[7] This seems to have been regarded as wasteful, and later texts have no such breaks, although a slight space may indicate a change of speaker within the line, as in a larger fragment of Euripides's *Hippolytus*,[8] or Menander's *The*

Sicyonians (*c.* 230–200 BC).[9] Exceptionally, such changes might be indicated by the use of colour.[10] If more substantial breaks, at the end of a strophe or a poem, were to be indicated, the *diple* or *coronis*, respectively a wedge and a 7- or reverse S-shaped mark, were used in the margin.

The earliest (third century BC) surviving fragment of Sappho exists as a pupil's exercise on an ostrakon, a shard of pottery, where the lines are fitted to the shape of the substrate.[11] A papyrus fragment of *Epicharmea*, a set of gnomic poems in trochaic tetrameters in handsome uncial script of about the same date, similarly preserves the lineation. The two tiny fragments now mounted below are from a play by Euripides and as early as the Timotheus papyrus.[12] The *Coma Berenices* of Callimachus (first century BC/AD) evinces a new characteristic, letters with serifs at the tips, written within ruled lines (except φ); the text lines are carefully spaced vertically and aligned to the left, with no distinction between hexameter and pentameter in the elegiac couplets; there is no word space, accentuation or punctuation.

The writing of dramatic texts for performance, at least as Aeschylus and Aristophanes had been performed, was now a thing of the past. This did not stop later Hellenistic poets from writing pastiche; one put anapaests, an ancient choric

Timotheus, *Persae*, papyrus roll, *c.* 400–300BC; from M.Norsa, *Scrittura Letteraria greca dal secolo IV a.c. all' VIII d.c.* (Florence, 1939), pl. Ia.

Sappho, ostrakon, *c.* 300–200BC; from Norsa, *Scrittura Letteraria*, pl.Vb.

meter, in the mouth of Cassandra in just such an anachronistic revival. The text is continuous, with no attempt at lineation, and the punctuation sparse. A horizontal line, visible two-thirds of the way down the left-hand side, may be part of a system of recording extent, as is the handsome signature letter 'A' in the right-hand corner. The script is regular and careful, some letters seriffed,[13] but without the self-conscious elegance of the famous epic 'Hesiodic Catalogue' of the heroines of Greek mythology, the hexameters neatly aligned, with occasional accents and breathings, but still without punctuation.[14] The roughly contemporary piece of Book VIII of the *Iliad* (Θ.433–47), however, is in script nearly as good, lineated, carefully accented and with breathings; there are points at the end of lines, as a guide to recitation rather than sense. A line left out by the original scribe has been scribbled in at the foot, evidence of contemporary editorial care.[15]

The sumptuous manuscript of the *Iliad* all in seriffed capitals, known from the place of its discovery as the 'Hawara Homer', was originally thought to be as old as our last two examples due to the presence of serifs like those found on stone inscriptions of the Augustan era,[16] until accounts datable to the early third century AD were found on the verso of the roll.[17] The presence, if irregularly, of all three of Aristophanes's accents, breathings, high and medial points, combined with the script, had all suggested an early date. Similarly, when the famous fragments of the fifth-century lyric poet Bacchylides were discovered in 1896,[18] they were again thought to be early, as they were also accented, with breathings,

Callimachus, *Coma Berenices*, ll.45–65, papyrus roll, *c.* 100BC–AD; Norsa, *Scrittura Letteraria*, pl.VIII .

Hesiodic catalogue, papyrus roll, 1st–2nd century AD; Berlin Staatsbibliothek, P.Berol. 9739 (W.Schubart, *Papyri Graeci Berolinenses* (Bonn, 1911), pl.19a).

Bankes Homer, papyrus
roll, 2nd century AD;
British Library P.114
(Lond.Lit.28).

and pointed; the letter-forms, the wide 'set' of the script and
generous (or wasteful) use of space seemed to point back to the
third century BC, and the layout, with uneven lines, seemed
again to put it close to the golden age of Alexandria. The lines,
however, do not correspond with the strophic structure (that is,
the arrangement of the odes in stanzas); such breaks are marked by
a simple horizontal *paragraphos*, with an asterisk to mark changes
in the metre. The same features now suggest an archaising scribe/
editor of the late second century AD. In addition to corrections
made by the original scribe, three other hands improved it, the last
two adding lines that the scribe had left out from another copy;
the marks for short and long syllables (two short diagonal strokes
and a single horizontal bar) were added to help comprehension of
a difficult text.[19]

Measurement of texts, by verses, lines and letters, is attested
both by contemporary writers and in surviving texts.[20] The
Bankes Homer, another imposing papyrus text of the second
century, has the verses numbered every hundred in the margin,[21]
and Menander's play *The Sicyonians* had the total number of lines
entered after the title at the end. A fragment of a manuscript of
Sappho in the Bodleian also gives the total, 1320 lines.[22] This
practice was essentially a matter of commerce as well as accuracy.
Scribes were paid by the line (the line as written, that is, not as
copied), and a line count enabled a price to be set in advance.
At the same time, it provided a guarantee that the work was

complete, so that the customer could not be short-changed by the scribe. Measurement, both of the completeness of the work and of its value for costing, was and remained a critical feature of the presentation of all texts. It was this, rather than any aesthetic preference for seeing and reading poetry in the form imposed by text and metre, that made scribes increasingly set out verse in the 'lines', metrical or rhythmic, in which poetry was composed.[23]

All the poems so far considered have been witnesses to the work of dead authors, many of them long dead. But some of the texts recovered from the sands of Egypt are near, if not contemporary with, their authors. Poseidippus, who wrote in the first century AD, was not a good poet, by any standards, but he wrote an elegy on old age, full of preposterous conceits (including a reference to the poem by Callimachus made famous by Cory – 'They told me, Heraclitus…') but not without a sense of humour or at least some self-knowledge; beside his text is a picture of himself as a statue, reading aloud his own works. Whether it was indeed he who wrote the text on a wax tablet (oddly laid out in two ill-balanced columns, in very uneven script), or whether (as Schubart thought) it was badly copied by a pupil, it is difficult to say.[24] Someone (could it have been Poseidippus himself?) decided that lines 11–14 at the foot of the first column were really too awful and, 'in a moment of grace', struck them out.[25]

A later scribe, book-collector and poet, Dioscurus of

Dioscurus of Aphrodito, acrostic poem, papyrus, 6th century AD; from H.J.M. Milne, *Catalogue of the Literary Papyri in the British Museum* (1927), pl.VII.

Aphroditos was, like Poseidippus, well aware of the possibilities of future fame offered by a written text. As a poet, acrostics, a purely visual device, were one of his specialities; in some, each stanza begins with the letter that is also the number of the stanza, a trick that would have appealed to Akkadian bards. He compiled a Greek–Coptic glossary, and preserved earlier works, among them Menander's *Samia*, which he copied, carefully punctuating it with colons and points. His own poems are written in a very sloped cursive, limping iambic trimeters on the left, more vigorous anacreontics on the right. They rather bear out Idris Bell's memorable judgement on him: 'His character may have been infamous, his personality certainly does not inspire respect, his verses indubitably merit damnation, but his services to papyrology are immense'.[26] There could be worse epitaphs.

Fragments of papyrus and, more rarely, vellum are not the only vehicle in which verse is preserved. Epitaphs and other inscriptions cut on stone are sometimes in verse, and epigraphic conventions, in which the presence or absence of verse had little influence, dictated a layout that was to influence the presentation of verse in other media.[27] Initially, the shape of the stone and the need to fill the available space overrode any feeling for poetic form. Distinguishing separate words with a medial point was, perhaps surprisingly, a common ancient practice in inscribing monumental texts; it may be Etruscan in origin.[28] Indentation was another ancient practice, whose object was to distinguish the line not indented.

The earliest Latin verse text to survive in what was once book form remains the papyrus fragment of a poem on the battle of Actium (31 BC) that was found at Herculaneum, thus written before the eruption of Vesuvius in AD 79. Written in a rustic script like the graffiti found at Herculaneum and Pompeii, it is

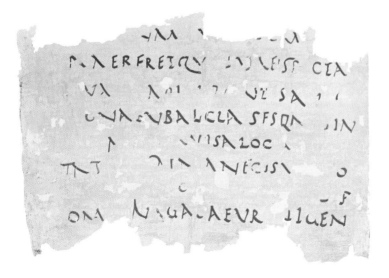

Poem on the battle of Actium, papyrus fragment, *c.* BC31–79AD; Naples, Biblioteca Nazionale, P.Hercolesi 817; reproduced from S. Morison, *Politics and Script* (Oxford, 1972), no 34.

Election notice, Pompei,
wall painting, *c.* 79AD;
M. della Corte, *Notizie
degli Scavi* (Naples, 1911),
no 31; reproduced from
Politics and Script, no 35.

wider in 'set' than most of them (the A, M and N are oddly reminiscent of the Bacchylides script). Each hexameter is set out on a separate line, medial pauses indicated with a *punctus elevatus*, or high point; a *paragraphos* or *coronis* like a sloped *T* or a λ on its side, inserted without any variation of interlinear space, marks sections. As in the inscriptions, the words are separated by spaces and punctuated with a medial point, a practice perhaps carried over from epigraphic convention. Seneca noted the practice, but it seems to have died out at the end of the first century.[29]

That this was in no way unique is demonstrated by a contemporary *graffito* from Pompeii, a 'vote for me' poster with the slogan as an elegiac couplet. The script is signwriters' rustic. The hexameter begins with a *littera notabilior*, the extra large letter beginning a word or chapter that came to be known as an 'initial' (the following I is naturally high – like the Hebrew *lamed* it makes a distinctive break in the otherwise even height of the script) and the pentameter is indented; the words are separated by the medial point. However, this was far from universal. The recently recovered fragment of the verses of the Roman poet Gallus (first century BC) from Qasr Ibrîm (first century AD) has the words unbroken, but the lines are separate, beginning with a strikingly large *littera notabilior*, and the pentameter again indented.[30] This practice has not been noted otherwise until the late fifth century fragment of Ovid's *Ex Ponto* at Wolfenbüttel.[31] The scribe of the famous fifth–sixth century Codex Bembinus of Terence's verse plays tries to maintain a stichic layout,[32] but is occasionally distracted by the length of the line and the need to squeeze in the first letter of the speakers' names in red; perhaps he was copying a rustic exemplar in *scriptio continua*. A later corrector, in the sixth century, put right one of these deviations using the *paragraphus* sign like a gamma on its side, and made the sense clearer by adding the 7-shaped divider, the *simplex ductus*. The same sign is used for a similar purpose in a third-century fragment of Livy's *De Bello Macedonico*.[33]

So far, we have seen little, apart from one or two fragments, but texts far older than their exemplars. The contemporary reader is not much in evidence, the author still less so, and the clouds now become thicker. But it is from this time, too, that the earliest manuscript books of poetical texts survive, some substantially complete, others only in fragments but still sufficient to imagine their original form. It is worth pausing to consider this paradox. What may be the earliest is the 'Ambrosian Homer', the *Iliad* preserved for its illustrations, whose capital script at first sight suggests a date not far from that of the Hawara Homer (that is, third century). More detailed consideration of the script suggests a date in the fifth century, a date confirmed by the illustrations. Illustrations apart, this must have been a spectacular piece of work, and it may well be that in layout as well as script it follows an earlier tradition, an exemplar of similar appearance. Where it was made is another matter (Constantinople, perhaps[34]), but it invites comparison with the 'Codex Augusteus', the earliest text of Vergil in as substantial form.[35] Both are lineated, and both without word-division or punctuation. Here the square appearance is artificially heightened by reducing the size of script for the last few letters of lines longer than the norm, so that the whole page fits within a simple square frame (the lines themselves have an upper as well as lower ruling). This sets it apart from another capital Vergil, also fragmentary, where the lines, also in *scriptio continua* but written as lines of verse, are full out to the left; high commas at the end of a line, added later, indicate pauses in the sense.[36]

Ambrosian *Iliad*, 5th century, vellum; Milan, Biblioteca Ambrosiana, F.205 inf.

VICIT INTERDVRVM PIETASDATVRORATVERI
N VT ET VAET NOTASAVDIRE ET REDDEREVOCES
ICEQVIDEMDVCEBAMINIMOREBARQVEFVTVRVM
TEMPORADINVMERANSNECMEMEACVRAFEFELLIT
QVASEGOTET ERRASET QVAIVTADERAEQVORAVECTVM
CCIPIOQVANTISIACTATVMINATEPERICLIS
QVAMMETVINEQVITLIBYAETIBIREGNANOCERENT

Vergil, Codex Augusteus, vellum, Italy, 4th century; Biblioteca Apostolica Vaticana, lat.3256.

Three other antique manuscripts of the national poet of Rome, one like the Ambrosian Homer illustrated, are of comparable splendour. All three date from the fifth century and are in rustic capitals (a national script, as capitals were not), and are pointed, but differently. The first, the 'Codex Vaticanus' or 'Mediceus', shows all three of the points prescribed by the fourth-century grammarian Donatus: the *distinctio* (low full point at the end of a sentence), *media distinctio* (mid-point after a completed clause) and *subdistinctio* (high point, our comma). This is the more interesting since a note (*subscriptio*) at the end records that this punctuation was added by Turcius Rufus Apronianus Asterius when he read it in the year that he was consul of Rome, 494 AD. Evidently, Donatus's rules for punctuation, which lasted, with some variation, for over a millennium, were already canonised as necessary both for the comprehension and for the recitation of verse. But the other two ancient Vergils, perhaps a little later in date, have only medial points between the words: the Codex Palatinus, perhaps the earlier, includes points only occasionally, the Romanus regularly. Like the Ambrosian *Iliad*, this last is illustrated; it too may be a literal copy of an earlier exemplar.[37]

These monumental books − codices, not rolls − are an indication of something new: the need for a more lasting record than the roll, whose be-all and end-all was the ephemeral task of reading aloud, in company or alone. The roll had only to answer the needs of the reader and the audience within sound of his voice. The codex made it possible to communicate the text to an indefinite number of readers, spreading over time and space. Their needs, real or presumed, dictated new disciplines in terms of layout, made possible by the form of this new thing, the codex, the book as we know it today. It was about this time that St Augustine surprised, and was surprised by, St Ambrose reading silently.[38] Neither was to know, though both may have surmised, the need that these books were going to serve. It is no surprise, however, that an even greater text, in their eyes, should have been similarly served.

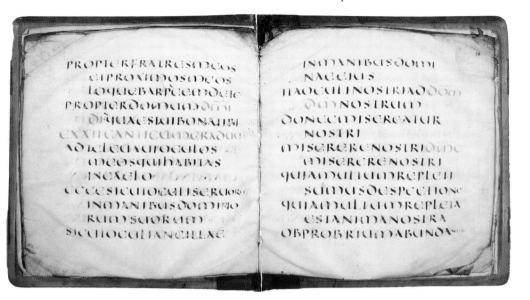

The other text to be given comparable status and form was the Bible, of which also three great codices survive. The earliest, the Codex Vaticanus, has no contemporary punctuation or division; Sinaiticus signals new paragraphs by extending the line where the break comes into the left margin; Alexandrinus goes further and marks the line with its first letter (not the letter with which the new section actually begins) enlarged and in the margin. These details (evidence, perhaps, of progress in time) concern us less than the treatment of verse, notably in the Psalms. Sinaiticus is normally written with four narrow columns on the page: for the Psalms, the number is reduced to two. The reason for the change is clearly to get each verse, wherever possible, within the line. Where longer verses run on, the second (and subsequent) lines are deeply indented (about 20 mm of a 128 mm line), the indent line vertically ruled like the columns. The first verse of each psalm is numbered in the left margin, each Greek numeral with a bar above and below it, both superscription and numeration picked out in red ink. Below the first line of each last verse is a sign like a sloping *T*, a combination of the *paragraphus* and *coronis*.

The reason for this complex arrangement was not only to make the text clearer: it also reminded the reader of intonation, familiar from the daily liturgy. Two needs had to be met, those of the reader and those of the performer. St Jerome was very interested in this. When confronted with 'difficult' passages of the Hebrew text, such as he found in Isaiah or Ezekiel, in which too he sensed the importance of intonation, he tried to make it easier by setting out his Latin *per cola et commata*, with a new line for each clause, like the speeches (he says) of Demosthenes or Cicero. Jerome had read Cicero well, and grasped the importance of a *clausula*

Psalter, 5th–6th century, France; Lyon, Bibliothèque de la Ville 425.

(punch line), the orator's need to provide aural aids to put across his argument. He was not alone in realising the importance of such auditory supplements as a means of understanding. When the need to protect the learning of the past persuaded Cassiodorus to set up the Vivarium at Squillace in southernmost Italy, he taught his monks punctuation by pointing an existing (but presumably unmarked) copy of the psalter, knowing that the breaks in sense and rhythm were already familiar to them, so that they would grasp the purpose of his notation. What such a book might have looked like can be guessed from the magnificent Psalter once at Lyon, written about AD 600, by a scribe 'schooled in the best Roman tradition' (Lowe),[39] but probably in France since the text is a mixture of the Roman and Gallican versions. Its square format betokens its antiquity, and the layout *per cola et commata* is conspicuous. There is no punctuation, apart from an occasional medial point in extra-long verses, but the titles of the psalms and any diapsalmata (interpolations in the psalmodic text) are in red, as are the *nomina sacra* (the divine titles, often abbreviated), which are followed by a point.

Codex Amiatinus, 7th century, Jarrow/ Wearmouth; Florence, Biblioteca Medicea-Laurenziana, Amiatino.

Just how successful this approach was can also be seen in the most Roman of early British books, the Codex Amiatinus, entirely set out *per cola et commata*. That Abbot Ceolfrid should have required three virtually identical copies, one each for his twin monasteries of Monkwearmouth and Jarrow and one to be taken back to Rome as evidence that the seed sown by Pope Gregory I had fallen on good ground, shows the high importance that he set on the layout of the text. But the most interesting tribute to Jerome's sense of the importance of visual appearance and its ability to assist reading, comprehension and performance can be seen in other, slightly later, Insular treatments of the same text in the eighth century. The psalter written early in the century, probably also Northumbrian, of which a fragment is now at Cambridge,[40] is clearly influenced by Ceolfrid's model; it has the same large initial letters, with the first line of each psalm full out left, but subsequent verses are economically run on, though with extra space before the first verse word. The slightly later psalter of which one leaf survives at Namur takes a different course: each verse begins with a *littera notabilior* set out into the left margin, while all the text lines begin evenly, with neither projection ('ἔκθεσις) nor indentation ('εἴσθεσις); the appearance is closer to Amiatinus, the practice more different. Another Insular psalter with Anglo-Saxon features at Basle runs both models further together, with a *littera notabilior* to begin each psalm inset into the text, and smaller initials, also within the text, for each verse. Another psalter from Echternach, now at Stuttgart, pursues the same line, but comes up with a different answer: the decorated psalm initials in Continental style and most of the dotted (an Anglo-Saxon trait) smaller verse initials are outset from the text lines, all beginning evenly. All this is clear evidence of the same line of thought pursued to slightly different ends.[41]

But all these occidental attempts to dignify and explicate the psalms and their liturgical use culminate in the Vespasian Psalter, made about AD 750, probably at Canterbury. This is an even more flattering tribute to the purpose of the Roman method

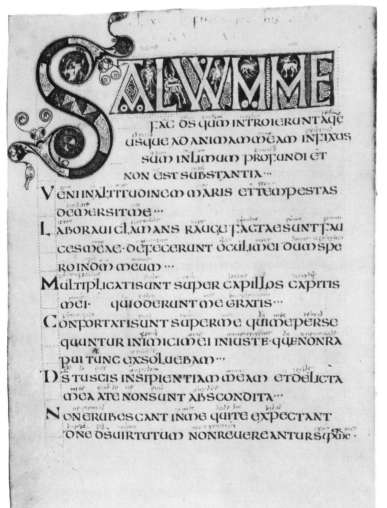

Vespasian Psalter, *c.* 750, probably Kent; British Library, Cotton Vespasian A.i.

of arrangement of text: the poetic structure was accentuated by stichic layout, as if it were metrical verse, with the classic system of punctuating verses or *sententiae*, with *distinctio, media distinctio* and *subdistinctio*, as well as the liturgical *punctus versus* (semi-colon). It also shows the insular practice of multiple commas (, ,,) to indicate pauses of different lengths, as well as initial letters outset into a margin defined by vertical dotted ruling. Verse initials are alternately red and blue. (This ruling, and the sequence of large initial followed by descending majuscules, are other Insular features, to which we will return.) In the Carolingian 'Palace Schools' at Tours, under Alcuin, at Reims and Aachen, the system was further refined and standardised: the large capital for the first word, first line in uncial, capitals for the first word of the verse, became standard. The demand for imposing psalters, bibles and other liturgical books repeated the same practice, which was echoed in the texts of the classics and other verse that date from the same period, while more decorative pages were also given a classical symmetry.

Bangor Antiphonary, 680–91, Ireland; Milan, Biblioteca Ambrosiana, C.5 inf.

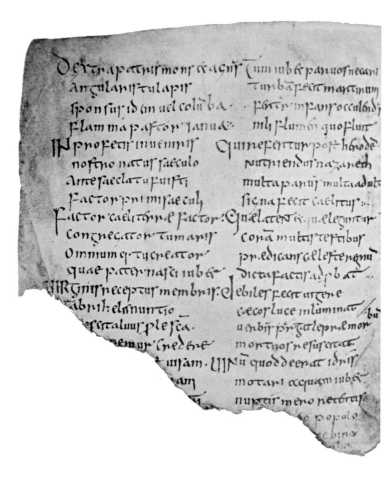

This long look forward over developments in the layout of the psalms is important since they underlie the shape and treatment of other kinds of poetry. The binary structure in the Psalms, inherited from even earlier texts from Mesopotamia, lent itself to antiphonal use in the liturgy, and that suggested the practice of using alternate colours for initial letters of verses. Communal use – St Hilary turned the divine injunction to sing into a hymn, 'Hymnum dicat turba fratrum', that makes its own point – is reflected in the earliest texts of the hymns that came to be added to the psalter and find their own place in the practice of the liturgy.[42] It may even explain the existence as well as the exotic shape of the bilingual Paris Psalter, and also extend to other forms

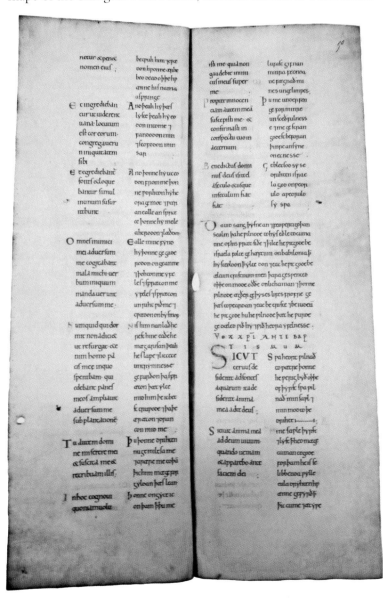

Paris Psalter, Old English, 11th century, perhaps Canterbury; Paris, Bibliothèque Nationale, lat.8824.

of verse with a similar structure.[43] The other form of dualism was the elegiac couplet, for which, as we have seen, the need to signal pairs of verses and the different metre of first and second lines was given early but not universal distinction.

This brings us to another influence, where again text and form had a mutual impact.[44] Verse epitaphs engraved on stone had their influence on the way that verse was written down, and *vice versa*. But the shape of monuments, the stones on which words were engraved, also had an influence. The title page of the Codex Amiatinus is consciously monumental.[45] The authority of Jerome's

Damasine inscription, 366–84; Rome, S.Sebastiano.

patron, Pope Damasus I, gave the inscriptions that he set up in Rome (still surviving, if recut) an influence perceptible now, even if obscured by the loss of many witnesses. The transition from monumental stone to scribal imitation of epigraphy, and from that to a manuscript equivalent, can easily be followed. The actual funerary stone that Charlemagne sent to Rome to commemorate the death of Hadrian I in AD 795 is in Latin elegiac couplets. But it was not cut in Rome; the engraver was Frankish and the writer was Alcuin of York. Although his model must have been manuscript, the 'Romanitas' of the inscription is unmistakable, even if the abbreviations and the Insular high T would not have been tolerated in its classical models.

The close relation earlier between inscriptions on stone and the inscriptional appearance of the early Vergils can only be surmised. If Vergil's epic is the earliest of the Latin classics of which witnesses survive, the next earliest is the satires of Juvenal. Two fragments, both sixth-century, show that copies as various as those of Vergil existed by then. One is a copy in formal uncial script; the other, preserved as wrappers for some papyri, and characterised by Lowe as 'the oldest specimen of a classical text in canonical half-uncial', shows that the text was lineated, although without word-space or punctuation of any kind.[46] The earliest texts by later poets, still classical but appreciably nearer in time to their first witnesses, fit in to the same picture. Prudentius's hymns survive in the manuscript in the Bibliothèque Nationale read by another literary Roman

CONTERATMEMBRISANIMUMQPASCAT
SPARSUSINUENASCIBUSOBSECRANUI
CRKISTICOLARUM

HYMNVSOMNISHORRE
DAPUERPLECTRUMCKORAEISUTCANANITIDELIBU
DULCECARMENETMELODUMGESTAXPTINSIGNI
KUNCAMOENANOSTRASOLUMPANGATKUNCLAUDEI

Consul, Mavortius, in AD 527. Just like the Codex Amiatinus Psalms, the first line of each verse is extended to the left (ἔκθεσις), but the words are unbroken and Mavortius, unlike Asterius, added no pointing. The metres of Prudentius's hymns are again those of classical lyric verse. The first hymn in lesser asclepiad is followed by a second in iambic dimeter catalectic, both identified as such by Mavortius. The metre in each is maintained by the lineation.

Prudentius, *Carmina*, 6th century, Italy; Paris, Bibliothèque Nationale, lat.8084.

There is, then, surprisingly little difference between a layout for the sacred page, as evinced in the Codex Alexandrinus and the Codex Amiatinus, and the earliest remains of books of secular verse. There was one important new distinction in the former, which brought about a rearrangement of text where a new section started: the large initial was now that of the first word in the new section, not the first word of the line in which the break occurred. We saw this transformation between the Codex Alexandrinus and Amiatinus, and we may wonder whether there was some connection here, and if so what suggested the change. That it was part of the evolution of the text as spoken, via *scriptio continua*, towards the text as seen, which needed intellectual markers rather than visual cues, cannot be doubted.

This purpose of the initial *littera notabilior* was new. The Augusteus Vergil reflects more ancient practice: the splendid initial A of 'agricolae' (Vergil, *Georg.* I.101) with chevron cross-bar opens the first word on the page; it reflects, not a break in the narrative, but the old scribal practice (perhaps originally a stichometric or measuring device) of marking the beginning of each new column, whether in roll or codex, with a large first letter.[47] This very book may have had a part in the progress towards modern 'initial' practice; it had early been in France, where it was recorded in the Abbey of St Denis in the fourteenth century, before Claude

Aureadaurticos enpingit littera cantus.
Ornarndecuit tambene tale melos.
Aureauer basonant promittunt aurea regna:
mansurum q; canunt & sine fine bonum.
Haec merito tabulis cultim decorant ebur mis:
quas mire exculpsit ingeniosa manus.
Illic psalterii prima ostentatur origo.
& rex docti loquax ipse canere choro.
Vt que decus redut sublatis sentibus olim.
quod fuerat studio peruigilante uiri.
Aurea progenies fuluo.   Lucidior auro.
carle iubar nostrum plebis & altus amor
Rex pie dux sapiens uirtute insignis & armis.
quem dec& omne decens quicquid in orbe plac&.
Exiguis famuli dagul fi sume lecborem.
dignanter docto mitis & ore lege.
Sic tua per multos decorentur sceptra triumphos.
dauitico & demum consociere choro.

Golden Psalter,
written by Dagulf for
Charlemagne to present
to Pope Hadrian I, *c.* 795;
Vienna, Österreichische
Nationalbibliothek,
lat.1861.

Du Puy gave it to Fulvio Orsini, and he to the Vatican Library.[48] The same A with chevron bar is repeated exactly in the Dagulf Psalter, appropriately in a book destined for presentation to Pope Hadrian I.[49]

There can be no doubt that the lessons of early classical, as well as sacred, texts were not lost on Alcuin, and that the form, as well as the words, of the epitaph of Pope Hadrian I owed something to one whose education had begun in York. The Damasine verses prefixed to the Vespasian Psalter are set out in a way that clearly indicates that a far earlier exemplar gave canonicity to layout and script, as well as text.

A copy of the Metrical Calendar or Martyrology, originally compiled at York in the second half of the eighth century, begins a collection, now fragmentary but probably written at Christ

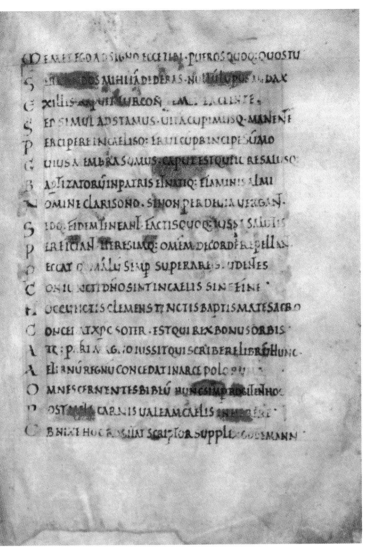

Benedictional of St
Æthelwold, *c.* 963–984,
Winchester, London,
British Library,
Add.49598.

Church, Canterbury, early in the ninth century. Each verse line
of the calendar begins with a *littera notabilior*, written concurrently
with the text, and here a change was made, which may be due to
what had already been done for holy writ.[50] The same is true of
the verses in the Benedictional of St Æthelwold, a hundred and
fifty years later, which combine an uncial *littera notabilior* with
respectably Roman, even Vergilian, rustic capitals.

Certainly, the Schools of Tours and Aachen showed the same
definite approach to the classical poets as to the Psalms. Like the
Vespasian Psalter, the initial letter of each verse of the Vergil
written at Tours *c.* AD 825–850 is enclosed in a square, ruled
off with a blind point from the text, in uniform minuscule. The
punctuation is for sense, not metre, and differs little from that
of the modern editor, with *punctus* for comma and *positura* for

full point. That this Carolingian format should also have been regarded as appropriate for John the Scot's stellar address to Charles the Bald, written about AD 877, is to be expected.[51] A list of similar examples could be extended indefinitely, but it is more interesting to pursue the exceptions.

What may be the oldest surviving fragment of Vergil is a school text in early half-uncial. Unfortunately, the more legible part is the Greek translation, but its layout is unusual by any standards. Each hexameter is set out on three written lines, with a *paragraphus* inserted every third line, where it is used to mark the end of each line of verse. There is also a paraphrase of the *Aeneid* of which only a papyrus fragment, fourth–fifth century, survives, found at Oxyrhynchus. In this, the lines were set out in pairs, two on the same line, here separated by a K, the ancient abbreviation for *caput* or *capitulum* used originally to indicate the beginning of a *periodus*, but later used generally to catch the reader's attention for all sorts of purposes.[52] This layout can be paralleled in a Tours manuscript of Boethius *De Consolatione Philosophiae*, written *c.*

Vergil, papyrus fragment, Egypt?, 4th century; Manchester, John Rylands Library, P.478.

Virgil paraphrase, papyrus, Egypt, 4th–5th century; Florence, Biblioteca Medicea-Laurenziana, PSI ii.142.

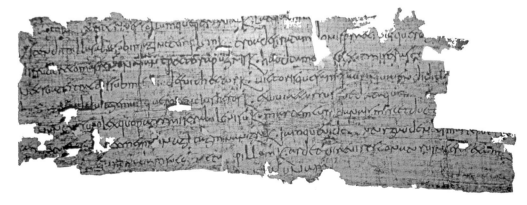

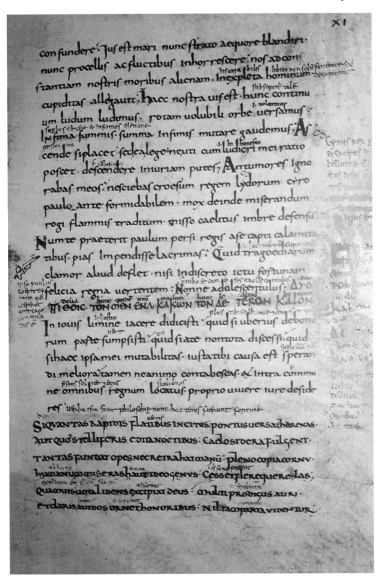

Boethius, *De Consolatione Philosophiae*, Tours, *c.* 850; Biblioteca Apostolica Vaticana, lat.3363.

850, in which the verse is again set out with two lines of verse to the written line: in this case, it is in a combination of lyric metres used by Horace (lesser asclepiad and phericratean), and the division between the two lines is marked by a *punctus elevatus*. It may be coincidence, or the accident of survival or of modern scholarship, but both this layout and the use of K seem to have English connections.[53]

A dual approach to layout was also carried in a different direction in another ninth-century Carolingian manuscript of Vergil.[54] Here the verses are not run on, but broken into two-line 'stanzas', so to speak, the first line marked with an extra-large *littera notabilior*, hovering between uncial and capital. The punctuation is sparing (a single medial point for all purposes), but follows the sense. The line breaks, on the other hand, are wholly aesthetic, with no consideration for sense or metre, even breaking a word occasionally. An entirely opposite contemporary approach can also be seen in inscriptional verse. The epitaph in elegiac couplets on the tomb of Gerbert of Aurillac, Pope Silvester II (1003), shows a determined reversion to classical standards, not only in the pure Roman capitals, but also in the layout, with the

Epitaph of Pope Silvester II, 1003; Rome, S. Giovanni Laterano.

couplets run on but divided by a point.

These examples are a reminder that the Carolingian formula for Virgilian Latin verse, which survives, more or less unaltered, to this day in print, was not the only one at the time at which it was canonised. Horace, by contrast, though known and quoted by authors in late antiquity, has no early witnesses, and seems to have been less known in the seventh and eighth centuries than his later imitators. It may be no coincidence that the earliest surviving MSS are no earlier than the ninth century. The oldest, now at Bern, was written by an Insular hand, more familiar perhaps with hymns (as in the Bangor Antiphonary) than classical lyrics; it is virtually unpunctuated.

The extent to which experimentation was possible is well demonstrated by a collection, Boethius *De Consolatione*, Persius, Prudentius and other works, written about 1100, formerly in the library of the Celestine convent at Avignon. The arrangement of Boethius's verse is no different from what it had been two centuries earlier, apart from the rubrication of initial letters of verse-lines, even when run on. The verse is no longer in half-uncial, but it is still written with two verse-lines to the written line, punctuated as such. The elaborate rubrication makes up for the absence of differentiation in the script. Later on, however, Prudentius's short lines suggested a new arrangement: it begins in two columns, still by no means normal for verse, and then suddenly breaks into three. The punctuation (triple point at the end of verses) is ancient, but the point at the right margin of every line reflects a new usage, as we shall see. If one page can be said to mark a turning point in the way verse was not only written down but imagined in visual form, this is it.

But already, Latin was not the only language in which verse might be composed or written. All this time, like the susurration

Boethius, etc, France, *c.* 1100; British Library, Add.15601.

of the distant sea that becomes a roar as you get nearer, verse in the vernacular is growing, filling people's minds, and, ultimately, emptying their inkwells, as the impulse to record it becomes stronger. The earliest recorded rhyming verse, and verse that depended on stress and alliteration, shows that methods of setting out the Psalter and Latin verse affected the layout of poetry that was now given visual form for the first time. If features that recall an earlier oral existence remain, it is no coincidence that systems of lineation and the use of *litterae notabiliores*, developed to meet the needs of liturgy or metrical voice, were adapted for quite different purposes. As with Greek and Latin verse, record, at least to begin with, lags far behind composition. Not only form, but words and the way that they were put together in the vernacular, were influenced by, and apt to be inextricably entwined with, Latin models. This was, again, a two-way process, and the volume and rate of traffic in either direction is hard to calculate, since the rate of loss is even higher than it is for other kinds of text. Tiberianus, least classical of later Latin poets, survives in a single copy; St Columban's enchanting verse epistle in adonics (a rare metre) to his friend Fedulius, which casts quite a new light on that turbulent missionary, is again unique; that there are as many as five copies of the *Hisperica Famina* is only due to its tantalising obscurity.

But echoes of contemporary speech, no longer Latin, can still be heard in all these. Influence in the other direction is easier to see. What makes it all the more fascinating – and again the analogy of the sea comes to mind – is that the composition, even the subject, of the verse is not so far off. The Siege of Troy is infinitely removed in time and space; the first record of it, the Ionian Greek version that Homer may have written, the Pisistratid revision in the sixth century BC, even the *Aeneid*, all are remote. Ker's *Epic and Romance* reached back beyond the texts to show how near the Volsungs, still more Burnt Njal, were to the bards whose prose or verse preserved deeds still within the memory of man. The mere difference between 'The Long Lay of Brynhild' and 'The Battle of Maldon' is evidence of it.[55] If it is the political consequences of the Viking inroads into France and England from AD 850 that tend to dominate our perceptions, confrontation left its mark on poetry in both directions.

3
And Back Again: Latin and Vernacular

One of the conspicuous features of Egyptian hieratic verse texts is rubrication, the picking out of the opening phrase, the pointing of the end of a line, in red. This was not a feature that could be replicated in cuneiform, nor did it find a place in Greek or Roman texts, not, at least, in those that have come down to us. But it found a place in the Eastern churches, liberally used in a seventh-century copy of the hymns of Severus of Antioch and a slightly later Coptic psalter. Both show the same interest in beginnings, the psalter with a larger first letter followed by others declining in size. Coptic inscriptions, too, reveal an interest in pointing between words,[1] which may also carry over from hieratic documents, although we have already seen that it was common in Roman inscriptions and such few early literary texts as survive. It is certainly found in the North African inscriptions examined by Mallon,[2] both in North Africa and Spain.

Whether manuscripts with either of these features found their way with the first missionaries to Ireland is an unanswerable question. But the earliest Irish manuscripts mark initial letters in some way, whether by enlargement (the other letters in the first

Hymns of St Severus, Near East, 7th century; British Library, Add.17134.

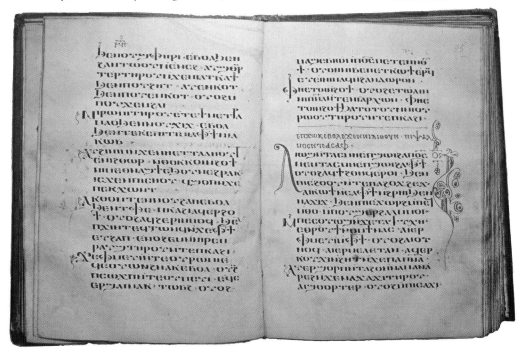

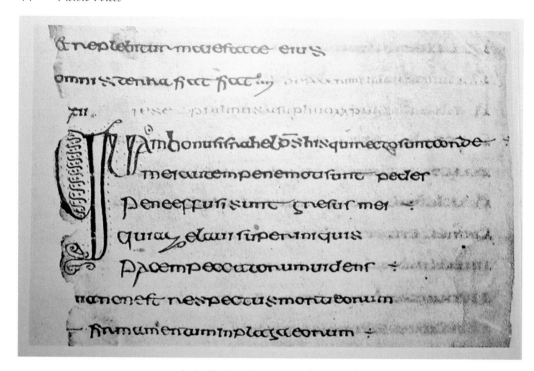

'Cathach', Ireland,
c. 550–600; Dublin, Royal
Irish Academy.

word declining in size, a feature that has been aptly called the Irish 'diminuendo'[3]), or the use of dots or colour. While none of these devices can be said to be peculiar to Irish or Insular manuscripts, they, or rather the reasons for them, were to have a significant effect on the way in which verse was set out. The Cathach was 'written in Ireland, traditionally, but not certainly, by St Columba',[4] therefore in the second half of the sixth century. For all its humble size and appearance, it is revolutionary in introducing word-division, and has the ends of stanzas marked with a cross; at the end of each psalm there is a line-filler made up of points ending in a 7-shaped *positura*, and the same strip appears as decoration beneath one of the initials.

The Bangor Antiphonary, *c.* 680–91, contains the text of St Sechnall's Hymn on St Patrick, originally written in his lifetime.[5] Its 23 stanzas begin with the successive letters of the alphabet in order; this is a noticeable feature of early Irish poetry, not an acrostic nor a form of numeration, but further evidence of fascination with visual form. The opening has a marked 'diminuendo' in red, which incorporates the red triple point used elsewhere as punctuation; the ends of stanzas are marked with the (three points or a point-and-7) *positura*. Nor were these phenomena solely Insular.[6] The cross to mark the ends of verses is also found in a limping ode on the achievements of the Lombard King Cunincbertus written about 700 in a version of the early minuscule later known to the earliest writers to take an interest in such phenomena as *litterae Langobardae*.[7]

The contemporary authority on punctuation and its techniques was Isidore of Seville; he is the first person to describe the *positura* (a mark at the end, rather than beginning, of a paragraph), and to identify its shape. It is found in a number of contemporary manuscripts,[8] which suggests that North Africa and Spain was the route by which it reached Ireland. In the general diffusion of previously held standards for the writing of certain kinds of text that resulted in the development of 'local' scripts, Irish reception and its graphic expression had a special place:

Ode to King Cunincbertus, North Italy, 8th century; Milan, Biblioteca Ambrosiana, C.105.

When the Irish first embraced Christianity their zeal for the Bible and the other written sources of Christianity led them to pursue a vigorous study of the Latin language, in which these texts were written. Since Irish is not a Romance language, its speakers tended to regard Latin primarily as a written or 'visible' language used for transmitting texts: they apprehended it as much (if not more) by the eye, as by the ear. Consequently, and perhaps further encouraged by observations that they found in the works of Isidore of Seville, they more readily perceived the written medium as a different manifestation of language with its own 'substance', and with a status equivalent to, but independent of, that of any spoken opposite number it may have had. The Irish regarded writing first and foremost as a means of recording information on the page, and they became the first to develop certain new conventions – features of representation and display – to facilitate access to the information transmitted in this 'visible' medium.[9]

There is a certain irony in the fact that the Irish, with an ancient language with a long tradition of oral transmission, should, in the process of adapting to a new religion and its practices, embrace and put to their own purposes grammatical devices made to assist the transfer of what was read aloud to what might now be read silently. But there can be no doubt that, whereas graphic devices were secondary to those who were still speaking Latinate if not Latin languages, they were of primary importance in Ireland, hence the need for a graphic supplement to the bare letters. The visual effect was critical, even if abbreviation and variety in letter-forms, the product of economic necessity, were frequent. The effects of this new outlook on the transmission of verse were considerable, particularly when they came in contact, if not conflict, with other ideas about graphic transmission prevalent at the same time in England and, in particular, in Northumbria. If Ireland had had to innovate, to adapt techniques devised for different purposes in various times and places in the Southern Mediterranean, the books sent by Gregory with Augustine came direct from Rome, and were copied in an uncial of inscriptional precision.[10] To reproduce it with equal precision was a duty undertaken with the same fervour that the Irish brought to copying the books that had come to them. The conflict in scribal attitude, as well as doctrine, was fertile.

Other manuscripts besides the Codex Sinaiticus had adopted a larger initial letter for the first letter of the first word of a new section, but the B of the first word of the Psalms in the Codex Amiatinus is not only larger than most; it was quite contrary to Roman practice.[11] It is not only the big initial, but also word-separation and punctuation that came from Ireland: the English contribution was to provide textual discipline to a system seen as purely visual in Ireland. The Insular style, thus developed, was to prove as influential in Europe (whence it had taken its sources), in the hands of Irish and English missionaries. It seems probable, therefore, that more than one of the disciplines that came to be used for distinguishing verse on the page originated in this fruitful antagonism of Northumbrian and Irish approaches. The result was no longer a single form, ancillary to the task of reading aloud, but several, each with its own purpose and its own self-descriptive apparatus. Old techniques, based on the needs of recitation and grammatical analysis, were maintained, but the new visual approach, a 'grammar of legibility', adapted them to its own needs, and evolved new ones. The Irish missionaries took their version to the Continent, where Dubthach wrote the hexameters of Priscian's *Periegesis* in 838 with first letters minuscule but touched with red.[12] But it was the English style – when St Boniface asked for a book written 'clare discretis et absolutis litteris',[13] it was Northumbrian uncial that he meant – that was canonised at Tours and Aachen.

To this complex must be added a further strand, oddly parallel to, if quite distinct from, the path that took uncial script from North Africa to Ireland and back to Northern Europe. Theodore, Archbishop of Canterbury (668–690), came from Tarsus, in

26

TENESCE SPECULATOR UERSI DI DIGNI DATOR HÆDDI
PIE PSUL PRECOR PONTIFICUM DITU DECOR ;PMETUO
PEREGRINO PRECES FUNDE THEODORO ·

Unius diei pretium de pane et aqua unus denarius demero
argento ualet paupi dare et potent iid; et ii paupib;
si panes cum potu et potent· et c xx solidos demero argen
to· pi an ualent· et palio xxii· et p· iii· xiiii· et pea reum
quisque inannoin· dies inebda· quia remissio ertc poeni
tentie a iii anno· usque ad finiaim numerum· uisi dniar
diebus et innatale dni· iiii dies et epiphania et inpascha· uiii d
et pente· dies quoque· sce marie· et sci michaelis· et xii aplou
et sci maram et illius sci quiuilla prouincia publice celebrat.
c· quoq solidos decocto auro promissis specialib; siue· cxx·
de argento puro; item malio loco scribitur· xxx denarios de
puro argento ualent prouina missa t iii· psaltoria cum xxx
palmatas idem ualent; item malio loco iudicatur· c psalmos inuerno ;

Theodore's verse letter to
Bishop Haeddi, *c.* 700AD,
Cambridge, Corpus
Christi College, 320,
f.154v.

Cilicia, his companion Hadrian from Libya. Both knew Greek,
and new evidence shows that they passed it on.[14] The rhyming
verse letter, 'Te nunc sancte speculator', that Theodore wrote to
Bishop Haeddi is in octosyllabic lines, but not in the familiar Latin
iambic but Greek trochees, the metre of the *Epicharmea* or, more
immediately, the anacreontics of Dioscurus of Aphrodito. He thus
set a fashion that lasted in Britain. Even more striking, the verse of
his pupil Aldhelm, the first written by a native Englishman, shows
him adapting a mind familiar with the old Northern practices of
alliteration and stress to Latin metrics; these traits are evident in
his hexameters, and more so in the continuous octosyllables that

he pioneered (iambic, unlike Theodore's trochees). That *Beowulf* itself may have been composed near Malmesbury is matter for further fascinating speculation.[15] Theodore's verse-letter is set out continuously in mixed capitals and half-uncial, and in red, as if intended as a heading to his prose 'Iudicia', which follow; the poem is, however, punctuated for sense. In the Book of Cerne, the poem 'Sancte sator suffragator' in the same metre, but rhyming at the half-line, written in Anglo-Saxon minuscule, is, remarkably, set out in half-lines, spaced horizontally (sometimes even splitting words) and vertically so as to accentuate the rhyme.[16] The long lines of the acrostic poem on the name of Aethilwald are set out as such. The great Vienna codex of the correspondence of St Boniface preserves four of Aldhelm's poems in rhyming, roughly iambic, dimeters.[17] The classical rules of elision are not obeyed, but the verses run across, two lines to the written line, punctuated with a space as well as a point. This is significantly different from the columnar layout of Theodore's verses. Aldhelm's lines are also

Book of Cerne, 'Sancte sator suffragator', Mercia, *c.* 820–840; Cambridge University Library, Ll.1.10.

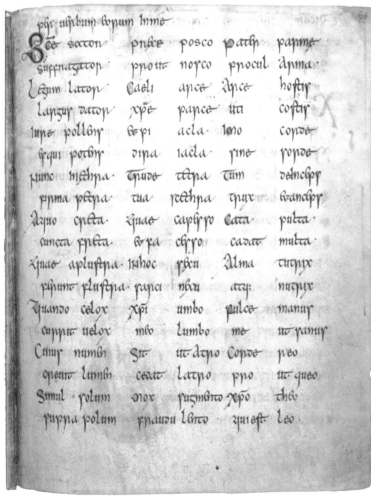

in minuscule, as are those of his pupil Aethilwald. There is an experimental quality about layout as well as composition in all these pieces.

About the middle of the ninth century, then, a number of events, more or less simultaneous, conspired to alter not only the face but also the function of verse. The Viking invasions brought epic, so to speak, home: not only the bards but the events they narrated were nearer in time. Fact became verse, and verse made myth of fact. Secondly, there was the collision between different kinds of diction: alliteration, metre and rhyme. Lastly, there was hymnody, the fitting of plainchant, used for non-metrical liturgical chant, to the metrical stanzas of hymns to make a repetitive tune. The hymns themselves might go back to Ambrose or Paulinus, but the melodies were new, sung antiphonally (at least in England).[18] Since all these features had coexisted for a long time – alliteration had come and gone since Ennius, stress had begun to shift the rhythms of lyric metre in the fifth century, and the existence of Germanic epic is attested in the sixth century – why was mutual impact so strong now? It may be that the determining factor was the writing down of verse for a readership for which Latin was increasingly a 'second language'. The sheer variety of medieval Latin verse, in metre as well as subject matter, needed more flexible rules for setting out texts. However, the universal popularity of epic and romance, in prose as well as verse, was not to be denied, and it is clear from the surviving examples that the existing systems for copying were soon adapted to meet the new demand. But the growth of verse in the vernacular went far beyond this; from 'The Owl and the Nightingale' to the *Divina Commedia*, new kinds of poetry, new types of texts, found an equal variety of forms.

If the most used (or most often found) Latin verse schemes, hexameters or elegiac couplets, lent themselves to Carolingian formalism, other schemes and other languages might or might not. Verse already familiar from chanting, such as the 'Te Deum', could be written in continuous lines with only an initial at the beginning of each stanza to signal 'repeats' in musical terms.[19] Other verse whose 'linear' pattern was not, perhaps, obvious also ran on, with punctuation only at the end of sentences. Nothing about the appearance of the famous manuscript of *Beowulf* suggests that it is a poem written in metrical verse, but the verse-lines are separated by points. The same is true of 'The Dream of the Rood', preserved in the Vercelli Book,[20] written in the tenth century, and we shall see that it becomes a commonplace in other non-Latin verse manuscripts. It is paradoxical that, deprived of the familiar Latin linear structure and with no inclination to ape it, scribes should yet have felt the need to signal a similar feature in a different and less conspicuous way. Perhaps by so doing they saw a way of avoiding the visual irregularity of rhythmic as opposed to quantitative verse. Elsewhere, in the 'Caedmon' manuscript,[21] for example, punctuation was added for elocutionary purposes, irregularly or regularly.

The roots of this 'squaring off' lie elsewhere, in inscriptional texts. The epitaph of Bishop Odemund, who died at Rome in 1074, is still in Roman capitals, but eccentrically spaced; the letters in the lower part, in particular, are aligned vertically to make the lines of even length. The change to Gothic script in the stone of Richard (d. 1289), notary to Pope Nicolas II, shows the same interest in filling the line as in the St Albans Psalter. The exceptionally fine new Gothic script on the foundation stone of the church of San Flaviano at Montefiascone dates from 1032, although recut *c.* 1300; here the leonine hexameters have been fitted in each on a single line and within the same lateral space, every abbreviation necessary employed to achieve a perfect rectangle. All these practices are of more than local interest.

The growth of hymnography was a phenomenon intricately involved in the development of the Christian church and its

Foundation inscription, San Flaviano, Montefiascone, 11th century, recut *c.* 1300.

liturgy. But its greatest exponent, St Ambrose, had been brought up on Horace, and his exquisite simplicity of diction combined with a subtle train of thought that could stretch over several stanzas were Horatian also in strict observance of metrical rules. Eleven of the hymns in the standard 'old hymnary' were by Ambrose, some included in the Vespasian Psalter.[22] Only slightly later, Prudentius observed the same sense of metre, and the layout of the early manuscripts of his works shows that the scribes were equally attentive (see above, pp. 34). Paulinus of Nola, besides writing elegiac couplets, could be equally Horatian, but his Northumbrian scribes hardly punctuated lines that ran on, regardless of the metre.[23] The most famous of all Carolingian hymns, 'Ut queant laxis…', whose first stanza provided the names of the notes in the octave, was written in sapphics of Horatian precision, set out as stanzas.[24]

The overwhelming new fashion for rhyme in Latin verse could be traced back to the Sequences, verses fitted for chanting in the liturgy. They became so familiar from liturgical performance that they could be set out continuously, with or without punctuation to point the rhyme-words. Indeed, it is hardly possible to think of rhyming *lines*: rhyme and assonance follow so fast on each other. On the other hand, the 'Cambridge Songs', however originally compiled in the Rhineland, were set out by their English copyist in two columns, the first letter of each song with a large initial, each four-line stanza with its own smaller initial, offset to the margin, and the lines, *aabb*, run on but punctuated. The effect suggests a monastic scribe (at St Augustine's, Canterbury) more used to writing liturgical or theological texts, who has applied his mind efficiently to an entirely different kind of text. A more complex system, the Victorine stanza (*aabccb*), has the short *a* and *c* lines run on, but the main *b* rhyme is signalled by breaking the line.[25] Alternatively, the *a* and *c* lines can be set out on separate lines, linked by a brace that leads the eye to the dominant *b*. The fascination with rhyme-systems of this sort could run away with

Paulinus of Nola, Carmina, Bibliotheca Apostolica Vaticana, Pal. lat. 235.

the scribe, resulting in the sort of layout that suggests a timetable rather than verse, the rhyme words, or more exactly the precise letters duplicated in each pair of rhyming lines, segregated in a separate column, with wavy lines guiding the eye back to the first part of each line. The afflicted eye is apt to lose its way when, as in the Oxford 'Troy' poem, the paired couplets are set out in rather tight double columns; an offset initial letter does not help much.[26]

The leonine hexameter is, by comparison, a noble instrument, especially in the hands of Bernard of Cluny, whose mastery of the metre in 'De Contemptu Mundi' avoided the easy temptation of rhyme-stopped clauses. Paradoxically, enjambement, with clauses crossing lines and a sentence stretching over three or more lines (an art of which Horace and Skelton were equally masters), encouraged visual presentation of verse-lines. The scribe of the earliest manuscript of the text was content simply to add points in the right-hand margin (note the double vertical ruling, a

Troy poem, shared rhyme-endings, France, 13th century; Oxford, Bodleian Library, Lat. misc.d.15.

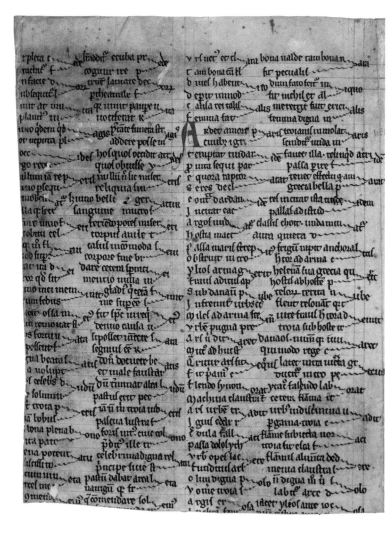

Urbs fyon. urbs bona. patia ofona. patia dulcis
do tua gaudia coroa fder pia duce. ducis
J erkm pia. patia ñ uia. pulch plare
do tua muñ fit tua detrā pitagorea.
Urbs fyon aurea. patia lactea. cue deora
Omne cor obruis. omnib obftruis 7 cor uor
Ñ efcio nefcio q̃ tubilatio luit t̃ glr
Quā focialia gaudia. glia q̃ fpali
2 aude ftuderis ea tolle meñf mea uicta fanfci
o bā glia uinco; moū lauf tua uina
$ f̃ fyon atia owibilantia martyre plen
c̃ ue micantia. pncipe ftantia. luce feren
Eft ibi pafcua mirib affua. pftura fer
R egif ibi thron. agminus 7 fon e epulanti
T enf duce fplendida. otio candida ueftib albi
$ f̃ fine fletib mfyon edib. edib almi
$ ūr fine crime 7 fñ thine ft fine litr
J mfyon aretb ediciomb uftir
P ar i floxida. pafcua miuda. uiua medull
Ñ ulla moletha nulla tgedia. lacma nt̃
O facra potio. fac refecto par animaru
O ton. opi o placid fon. ymn earu
$ ufficiens ab e 8f omib ipe redempti
P lena refecto ipa uifio cunctipotiñs

Bernard of Cluny, *De contemptu mundi*, France, 14th century; British Library, Add. 16895.

remote descendant of the Vespasian Psalter pattern). The second scribe, however, carefully noted the internal rhymes, as well as picturesquely linking the rhyming lines with a pair of red lines leading to the last letter, placed full out right. The third scribe uses alternating initials to the same effect, and has a wider battery of punctuation, using both *punctus versus* and *elevatus*.[27] Other famous medieval Latin poems attracted much less visual accompaniment. The scribe of the 'Arundel Songs' ignored not only punctuation but any semblance of the Goliardic rhythm in writing out 'Dionei sideris favor elucescit / et amantum teneris votis allubescit', while 'Naturae thalamos intrans reseransque poeta', a poem that seemed to C.S. Lewis the culmination of the 'allegory of love', only survives, a patent afterthought, squeezed in the extra-wide margins of an earlier anthology.[28]

The very early vernacular verses in German and French may have conformed to the Carolingian pattern simply because no other occurred. But most of the early verse texts in French, German, Italian, Provençal and Catalan were written continuously, with or without punctuation to help the reader find the rhyming lines. Whether this was due to economy or a feeling that such light matter did not merit larger space and materials, or whether (as is clearly sometimes the case) the copyist was unaware that what he was copying was verse – these questions can only be answered case by case.

Yet the visual links between old and new are revealing. That earliest of German romance texts, the early-ninth-century *Hildebrandslied*, was written on blank leaves of a collection of biblical texts written at Fulda in an Insular hand, *c*. 830–40. The German text is written accordingly as prose, with a single point at the end of each verse-line; the script is the plainest Carolingian

Hildebrandslied, Germany, 9th century; Kassel, Murhardsche Bibliothek.

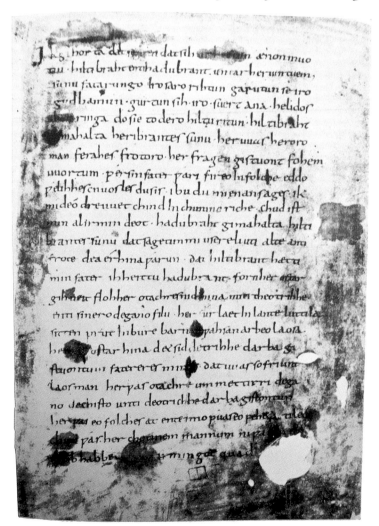

DE POETↄ

Dat χ fregin ih mit firahim
firi uuizzo meista· Dat ero ni
uuas· noh uf himil· noh paum
noh peregniuuas· ninohheinig
noh sunna ni stein· noh mano
niliuhta· noh dermæreo seo·
Do dar niuuiht niuuas enteo
ni uuenteo·⁊ do uuas der eino
almahtico cot· manno miltisto·
⁊ dar uuarun auh manake mit
inan· cootlihho geista⁊ cot
heilac· Cot almahtico du
himil⁊ erda χ auopahtor·

⁊ du mannun so manac coot
for χpt· for gipmir indino
ganadec sehta galaupa·
⁊ cotan uuilleon· uuistom
mi spahida⁊ craft· tiuflun
za uuidar stantanne·⁊ arc
za pi uui sanne·⁊ dinan uuil
leon za χ uurchanne·

Qui non uult peccata sua penitere
ille uenit regum ubi iccmamplius
illum non penitebunt· nec illorX
se ultra erubescit·

minuscule, with, however, traces of Insular influence. The Wessobrunn 'Creation Poem' is even earlier, written in a more handsome Carolingian minuscule, surprisingly large for so small a page; it too appears on two pages of a theological commonplace book, attributed by Bischoff to the abbey of Staffelsee and datable before 814. It follows the style of the rest of the book in its use of capitals, but the verse lines, though run on, are punctuated, not only with a final *distinctio*, but also medial *subdistinctio*. It is altogether a more sophisticated performance, heightened by the uncial heading (perhaps an afterthought). But both of these seem to have acquired their appearance by accidental association with pre-existing texts.[29] The *Evangelienbuch* of Otfrid von Weissenburg is a very much more substantial performance, written about 865 by one main scribe, with at least three others, one of them Otfrid himself. He used a ballad metre (strongly stressed rhyming trochaic octosyllables), and both layout and punctuation show that the line-pairs follow the age-old pattern of the Psalms.

In the Frankish kingdoms, early poetry in old French was written down along with German. The fascinating bilingual verses preserved at Valenciennes were written by a skilful scribe, familiar with Carolingian Latin orthodoxy in the matter of writing out verse. Writing in two languages, old French and German, presented no problem. The rhymes (more complex in French than German) were set out in the same way, on a single line. The French metre (dactylic) and rhyme is treated in the same way as Otfrid's text, with a point to separate the two rhyming halves, the second 'answering' the first, as in the Psalms. The shorter, rougher German lines are (after a false start) set out as quatrains,

Wessobrunn 'Creation Poem', Staffelsee, Germany, *c.* 800; Munich, Bayerische Staatsbibliothek, Clm 2053.

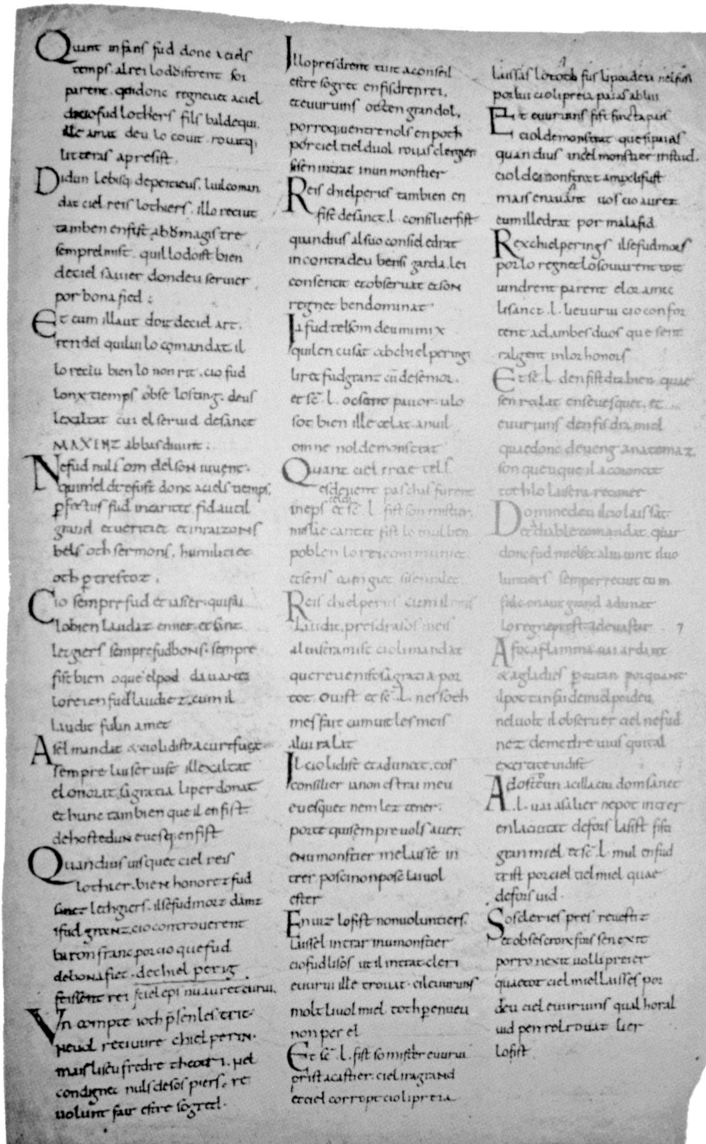

'Vie de St Léger',
Southern France, *c.* 980;
Clermont-Ferrand,
Bibliothèque Municipale,
189/240.

as if they were elegiac couplets.[30] The earliest purely French text, the 'Vie de St Léger', comes from a collection of early vernacular texts, now bound together as an album, at Clermont-Ferrand. It resembles Otfrid's paraphrase of the gospels in appearance, though the page is larger and in two columns. The fine southern Carolingian minuscule is as easy to read, and the alternating capitals to each stanza add to its liturgical appearance.[31]

The 'Chanson de St Alexis', an integral part of the St Albans Psalter at Hildesheim, cannot be accused of economy, either. In addition to the elaborate initial at the beginning of the text, each stanza begins with a *littera notabilior*, and alternate written lines are in different coloured ink (but these bear no relation to the verse

'Chanson de St Alexis',
St Albans, *c.* 1200;
Hildesheim, St Godehard.

lines). The earliest Italian text is on the same subject, a *ritmo* on the life of Sant'Alessio, in a dialect curiously similar to modern Sardinian.[32] It is written continuously, in a documentary rather than book-hand, and only occasionally punctuated at line ends. The stanzas are of irregular length, in trochaic dimeters, each stanza with the same rhyme throughout. The earliest Spanish, or rather old Castilian, text is the 'Razon de Amor' of Lope de Moros.[33] This is also in a documentary hand, heavily abbreviated and unpunctuated; the rhyming couplets are in a roughly trochaic metre, with acatalectic dimeter as the norm but with much variation. Unusually, the written lines follow the lineation of the poetry, but often run on when the sense suggests it. If some way

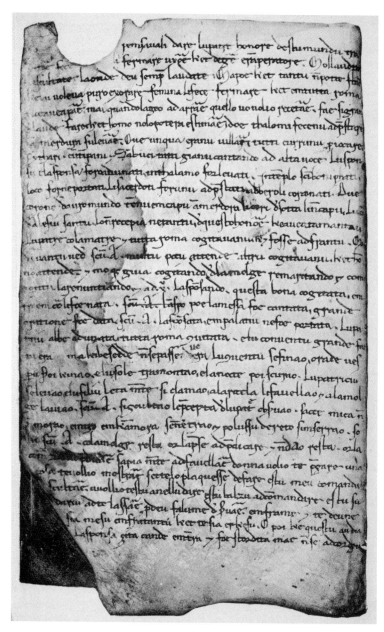

'Ritmo di Sant' Alessio', Santa Vittoria in Matenano, *c.* 1180–1200; Ascoli Piceno, Biblioteca Comunale, XXV. A. 51.

from the poet's hand or voice, this is not as remote as earlier examples, closer to the classical or liturgical texts more familiar to their writers.

Even closer, perhaps, is the minstrel's song, hastily scribbled at the foot of a canon law text written in the twelfth century, probably in Florence (it was once at the basilica of Santa Croce).[34] The poem itself, in the same metre as the ballad of Lope de Moros, offers panegyrics to a series of ecclesiastical potentates, and must have been written itself about 1200. The form is largely dictated by the available space, but the lines are carefully if irregularly punctuated, and the two stanza breaks are marked with a *paragraphus*.

One genre of verse that was never so treated, and for which its own layout and rules were developed, was the *chanson de geste* and other verse 'romances'. The myth, romantic itself, that the earliest surviving texts of these romances originated with their authors, and these rough undecorated books were 'jongleurs' copies', has been effectively despatched.[35] It was not just elaborate books, however, like the 'Vie de St Alexis', but even the first text of the *Chanson de Roland*, a humble piece of work, that came to be written in England, and within the general context of monastic copying. Similarly, the oldest French text with rhyming verses, the 'Chanson de St Foy', was written at the Benedictine abbey of Fleury.[36] If the jongleur depicted in the romance of 'Tristan' was a master of the 'gai saber', his text, the first letter of each rhyming pair offset, the second indented, was a soberly professional piece of work.[37]

The two-column layout, increasingly preferred now for all kinds of prose, is another sign of the rising status of verse, in particular the newly popular genre of romance.[38] The short octosyllable lines encouraged further formalisation: three-column, and later even four-column layouts came in, with still more elaborate ruling. A ruled space marked by piercing with a point made it possible to lay out several 'sheets' at once, ready for writing, the holes at the end of the right-hand column on the recto becoming those for the initial line of the left-hand column on the verso. The lunar reflection of this last encouraged page-layouts with a punctuation mark at the end of the line (such as appear in the earliest manuscript of Bernard of Cluny), round which the flourishes of the cadels are wound; punctuation and decoration, never far apart, are here very close. It was an easy step from this to the practice of making up

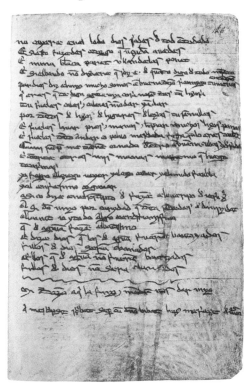

Lope de Moros, 'Razon de Amor', Aragonese, 13th century; Paris, Bibliothèque Nationale, lat.3576, f.124.

Minstrel's Song, *c*. 1200, Italy; Florence, Bibliotheca Medicea-Laurenziana, Santa Croce XV.6.

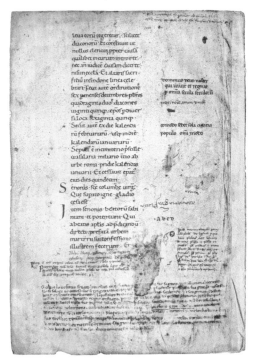

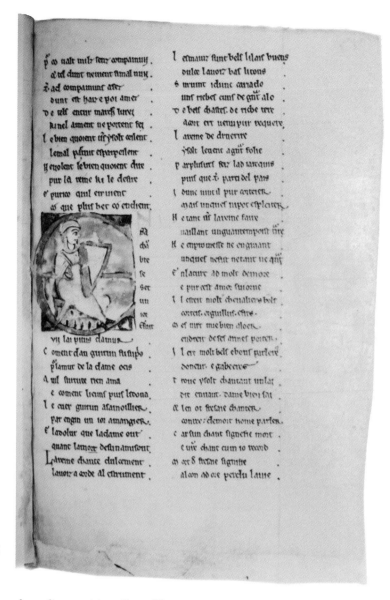

Romance of Tristan,
c. 1200, Southern England;
Oxford, Bodleian Library,
Fr.d.16, f.10r.

short lines with a line-filler, executed by the rubricator in the manuscript of Anglo-Norman poems, *c.* 1300, by 'Maistre Gacé'. The ruling includes an extra bounding line to the left of the column as a guide for the *litterae notabiliores*. This is much more easily seen in the copy of 'Athis & Porfilias', dated 1330, written for 'Jeanne de Chastillon, fille de Gautier, Connetable de France, femme de Gautier Duc d'Athenes et Comte de Brienne'. The triple ruling, clearly marked with plummet, is aligned, 'backed up', with that on the verso (so that the 'L' on the other side is clearly visible).[39]

In the fine illuminated 'Roman de la Rose' the mechanical process of ruling is put to another purpose: the right-hand bounding

Athis et Porfilias, 1330, France; British Library, Add. 16441.

Roman de la Rose, 14th century, France; British Library, Add. 31840.

line of the left column acts as a marker for the illumination of the right column; the implied line is carefully observed for the smaller *litterae notabiliores*, and the initial letter of every second line is touched with red to emphasise the rhyme. Sometimes the last letter of the line was extended into the regularly demarcated space for the text; scribes more used, perhaps, to the carefully justified columns of prose obviously missed the even right-hand margin. The effect of the extended letters may have been to serve the same purpose as catch-words, imitating the chanting voice pausing, with perhaps a melisma, a cadenza for the voice, on the last rhyme-word.

Both format and text had now become the preserve of professional scribes, such as Guyot who worked for Chrétien de Troyes. Script and the space delimited for it were laid out with geometric precision. The octosyllabic lines, with two, four or even eight lines rhyming together, moved at such an even pace that punctuation was hardly necessary and rarely supplied. Space was the only variable: when the short line was new, the layout was wasteful of vellum, and the immediate move to three columns produced a cramped page; but in Guyot's hands three columns could be fitted elegantly as well as economically.[40] There were exceptions to the punctuational void. In the 'Bible historiale' of Herman de Valenciennes, in alexandrines, the caesura is regularly marked with a mid-point. But so little relevant did the old techniques now

Gautier de Metz, *L'Image du Monde*, 1342; British Library, Royal 20 A.III.

seem that a copy, written in 1342, of Gautier de Metz's 'L'Image du Monde' has alternatively point and *punctus elevatus* at the end of successive lines, thus reducing to mere decoration what had earlier been its counterpart.

The survival of early Middle English verse, like the Latin verse in the Arundel Songs, seems hardly to have been visually dependent on its recognition as such. The *Ormulum* looks like what it paraphrases, an economically written evangeliary.[41] Layamon's *Brut* was either mistaken for (or treated as) a prose chronicle: 'the verses are end-stopped, but in both surviving manuscripts they were copied continuously across the column, with hemistichs and verses separated only by punctuation'.[42] Only the caesura remained to identify it as verse. This is the stranger since the

'The Owl and the Nightingale', *c.* 1250, England;
Oxford, Jesus College, 29.

earlier of the manuscripts also includes 'The Owl and the Nightingale', laid out and clearly recognised as verse.[43] These texts are early thirteenth-century, but a collection of sermons written *c.* 1400[44] contains stanzaic English verse, quoted within Latin prose and run on with it without distinction. The famous lyrics in Harley MS 2253 ('Bytuene Mersh and Aueril', 'When the nyhtegale singes' and the rest) are partly lineated, partly not.[45] In the *Polycronicon* John Trevisa translated Ranulf Higden's Latin verse chapter on Wales into English verse, lineated as such; other passages similarly translated as verse are written as prose. The many manuscripts all repeat this distinction, so presumably the difference goes back to Trevisa's original.

Other factors may be at work here. In the University Library, Cambridge, there is an elegantly written verse collection of lives of female saints.[46] It is a little book, with the text run on as if in prose, although the verse lines are marked with a decorative initial. Is this due to the small format (books of hours are similarly written with a minimum of breaks in the text), or does it indicate the preference of the women for whom it must have been written? The trend can operate in reverse. The 'romance' layout with

Lives of female saints,
15th century, England;
Cambridge University
Library, Add.4122.

Harley Lyrics, *c.* 1330–40, England; British Library, Harley 2253.

offset first letters to each line was an Anglo-Norman invention that was easily extended into English verse. Marking the stanzas with a paraph was a natural development of the by now familiar formula for Chaucer's newly introduced rhyme royal to have its stanzas marked with a paraph. Similarly, Langtoft's Anglo-Norman chronicle has passages at the end in English tail-rhyme, shorter than the main octosyllables, with the second rhyme-pair indented to the right. The bob and wheel in 'Sir Gawain and the Green Knight' are there to separate the rhymed and alliterative lines.[47] The great success of Chaucer created not only a pattern, a yardstick by which the right way to present verse in English

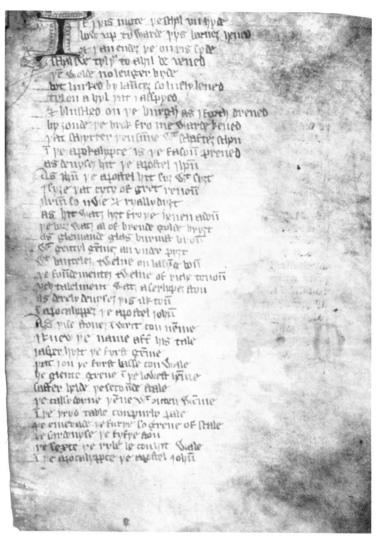

'Sir Gawain and the Green
Knight', late 14th century;
British Library, Cotton
Nero A.x.

could be measured, but also a book trade able to meet it. Outside
London older practices prevailed. The 'Pricke of Conscience'
written at Bolton in 1405 has each first letter picked out in red
(but not offset), while the rhyme pairs are braced at the end as they
had been a century earlier.[48] The complex and irregular rhyme
scheme of the romance of Octavian the Emperor required festoons
of brackets to pick out the rhyming lines; curiously, no other
punctuation seems to have been thought necessary, although the
rubricated initial letters are evidence of careful preparation.[49] The
well spaced elegant lines of the presentation copy of Hoccleve's
'De regimine principum / The Regement of Princes', made for
Henry V as Prince of Wales, has none of these traits: this was the
work of a London trade by now as professionally equipped to
present English verse as the Paris trade French romances a century
earlier.[50]

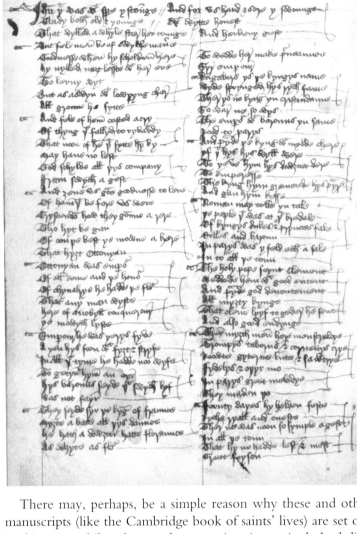

'Octovyan Imperator',
15th century; British
Library, Cotton Caligula
A.ii.

There may, perhaps, be a simple reason why these and other manuscripts (like the Cambridge book of saints' lives) are set out in this way, while others at the same time increasingly look like 'poetry books', as we would expect them to look. The fifteenth century was a time of increasing social and political change. Recovery from collapse after the Black Death was complete. The balance of power between France, England and Burgundy swung with alarming rapidity. The economic resources of Germany and finally Spain began to have a measurable impact. The maritime nations, particularly Venice, encouraged and profited by these changes. For all these reasons, conventions in the form and presentation of texts were questioned and some changed. The rule of the two-column layout was broken increasingly often, in prose and verse. So, if Gower's long octosyllabic lines remained firmly in two columns, Chaucer's more variable metres and

And although yt be no maner of neede
zow to consylle what to don or leue
zyt If zow lyst of storyes taken heede
Sum what yt may pfyte by zou leue
At burdest whan ze ben in chaber at ens
They ben good for to dryue forth the nyght
They shal nouzt harme If yoy be herd a ryght

To zour hyness thynk yt nouzt to longe
Thogh in that draght I sum what wade deps
The theses venous that to yt longe
Wachen my gost and letten hym to sleepe
Now god in vertu zow maputene & kepe
And I beseche zowr magnificence
zeue on to me benigne audience

For thogh I to the steppys clergial
Of thise clerkes thre nat may atteyne
zyt for to putte in ps my conceyt final
Good wyl me artyth take on me the peyne
But þre in me ther gwappyth euy weyne
So dredful am I of myn ignorance
The crois of crist my werk speed and avance

Aristotle. Giles. Iacob.

Explicit prologus
De principio regie Incipiendo & fide observanda.

Now gracious prince a geyn that the corone
honoure zow wyth ryal dignite
By secheth hem that sit an hye in trone
That whan that charge receyued han zee

stanzas were more often in one. This was in both cases the result of commercial development, as the market for professional copies expanded. Gower's lines fitted a standard 46-line page, while the glosses added to Chaucer required and got a more spacious page; by a further development, Lydgate's Latin marginal glosses gradually merged with the text columns.[51]

Some of the complex pressures at work here almost simultaneously can be seen in the evolution of 'Piers Plowman'. Its alliterative stressed lines were a conscious revival that did not fit Anglo-Norman geometry. The early texts are thus written in the distinctive *anglicana* book-hand, each verse on a separate line, first letters irregularly capitalised, with a prominent red point at the caesura. The different sections of the text, such as changes

Opposite Thomas Hoccleve, *De Regimin Principum*, 'The Regement of Princes', early 15th century; British Library, Arundel 38, f.39v.

Left 'Piers Plowman', 15th century; British Library, Cotton Vespasian B.xvi.

of speaker, are marked with a paragraph at the beginning, and (surprisingly, since it reflects 'romance' style) with a wavy line-filler at the end. The later texts, however, have conformed to the 'trade' pattern; one at least of them has the verses run on as if prose. Thus, while in other instances English verse was late to emerge as visually distinct from prose, 'Piers Plowman', perhaps because of its archaic style, moved contrariwise from linear to continuous form.

We tend to take for granted the survival of poetic texts in English, French and Anglo-Norman, but what has come down to us, if exceptional compared with those in Germanic or other romance languages, is still only a fragment of the whole. One of the areas of greatest loss has been the anthologies of *Minnelieder* and the songs of troubadours, the latter due to the disappearance of Provençal and the '*langue d'oc*'. The survival of the 'Chansonnier

Chansonnier Occitan, 15th century, Provence; New York, Pierpont Morgan Library, M.819.

Occitan' is unique, not only in language but also in the diversity of its contents.[52] Such books suggest that every possible kind of transcriptional form was used, prefiguring more personal anthologies. Great men who were also famous in their own time as poets, such as René d'Anjou, King of Provence, who wrote equally in French and Provençal, or Charles d'Orléans, who was a prisoner of war in England and was also bilingual, could command a masterpiece of script and illumination at public level, so to speak. But these were display pieces; both they and lesser men and women kept collections of songs and poems, written for their own use, sometimes even by them. The 'chansonnier' of Charles d'Orléans was not only less imposing but more various in its content.[53] Other lesser personages, such as Richard Hill, Adrian Fortescue, or a man called Rate, compiled books of verse,

Charles d'Orléans, Poésies, *c.* 1483–1500; British Library, Royal F.II.

prose extracts, and other memoranda – a personal anthology of a sort that would have been unthinkable a century earlier.[54] One-off, one-man or one-woman books have probably survived less than other more visibly 'library' books. That they have survived in the numbers in which they have is evidence of a new trend in the making as well as ownership of books.

Rate's book is, to our eye, oddly narrow, and 'agenda format', here as elsewhere, may have originated in pocket notebooks, diaries or account books. It makes a difference from the traditional 'book shape', which we have seen move from the square format of the great codices and the Lyon psalter *c.* 600 to the familiar oblong of today. But narrow books, which had the advantage of saving the quantity of vellum needed to write them on, date back to the twelfth century, especially for Latin verse texts for university

Horace, Odes, *c.* 1200; Barcelona, Biblioteca Nacional de Catalunya, 1815, f.7.

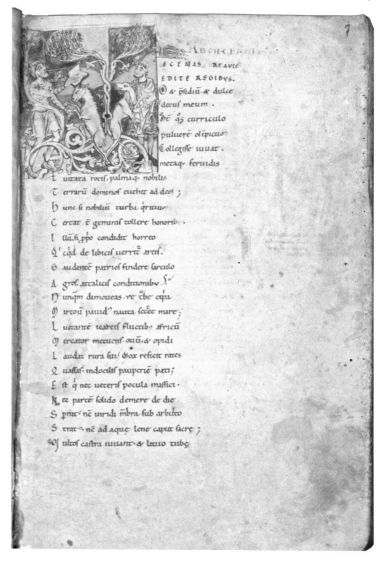

use; this enchanting Horace from the Biblioteca Nacional de Catalunya, with the poet disporting himself with goats round the Bandusian spring, would have been one of them. The use of verse for didactic purposes, whether as university texts or for school use, or simply as a help for the autodidact, is ubiquitous; remembering, the primary function of the features that distinguish verse and poetry from speech and prose, is also the purpose of instructive verse, whether its subject be astronomy, grammar or poetry itself. The long process of evolution, from simple marginal note to a substantial commentary, that brought about the 'gloss', that most influential of medieval (and earlier) literary forms, influenced the shape of the verse that it not infrequently accompanied. A gloss, in Latin or vernacular, might sometimes act as paraphrase or even as a substitute for translation.

'Whatever is the use of a book without pictures', said Alice, echoing an age-old demand. Pictorial images, added to as well as in verse, have amplified its words in memorable ways since the Vaticanus of Vergil, memorably enlarging the text of romances,

Lydgate, 'The Fall of Princes', 15th century; Manchester, John Rylands Library, Eng. 1.

the works of King René and Charles d'Orléans, and most of all the prolific and ever popular John Lydgate. But long before printing made it a necessity, taste, or economy, began to move away from colour: *grisaille* (monochrome) emerges as an alternative to coloured pictures, red and blue paragraphs and cadels become rarer. The individual scribe became the sole master of his page, solely answerable to his patron's taste, or his own, as more people began to write books for their own use. Even those who could afford otherwise, such as the customers of David

Ponthus et Sydoine,
15th century, France;
Cambridge University
Library, Ff.3.13.

Aubert or Jean Miélot, both booksellers as well as professional scribes, chose penwork decoration.[55] The scribes responded with imaginative explorations of the new opportunities and new space thus opened to them. The copyist of an anonymous French romance, *Ponthus et Sydoine*, decorated his page with quite extraordinary penwork initials incorporating legends which are in effect the moral of his text.[56]

This is yet another reminder of the mnemonic function of verse. Devices like this are sophisticated examples of it, but they are a reminder that punctuation, ruling and all the other basic tools for laying out a text were mnemonic too. Grammar itself, evolving over almost as long a period as the texts it analysed, also had to be remembered, and verse had its part in that. The *Doctrinale* of Alexander de Villa Dei was a Latin grammar in verse, and one of the most popular of all medieval texts, in terms of survival, if not with those who had to learn from it. Its rhymes must have been as familiar as the lists of prepositions governing the ablative and accusative in Kennedy's *Latin Grammar*, and its tabular structure helped many, like Sir Grummore Grummersum, to remember the rules by reference to their visual appearance. The popularity of the *Doctrinale* lasted into the early years of printing, and fragments, some on vellum, of lost editions exist, as they do of the older and still more popular Donatus. Like all grammarians, Alexander was interested in exceptions, and this links his work with another poet, who has one unique claim to fame.

Johann Borne was the first author to see his own works in

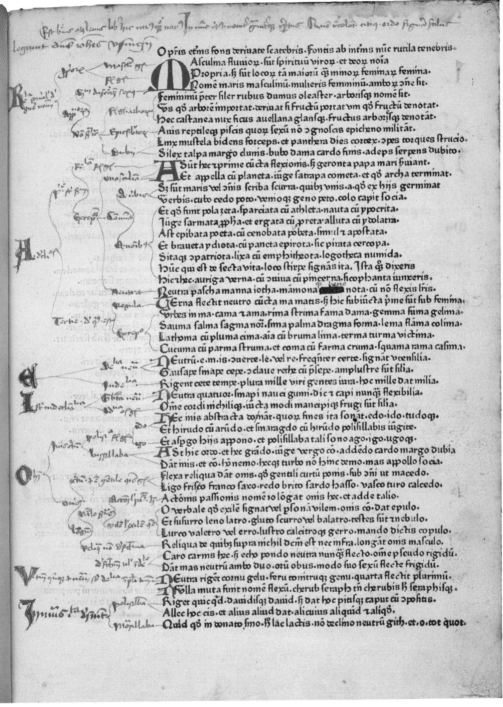

print. He owed this distinction to his employment as editor and proof-corrector at the press of Johann Fust and Peter Schoeffer, in which capacity he (I believe) witnessed the Helmasperger Instrument in 1455, the critical document in the earliest history of printing, in which the partners in it divided up the spoils. But

Johann Borne, *Grammatica Rhythmica*, Mainz, *c.* 1468; Manchester, John Rylands Library.

Borne has a greater claim to fame as the first person to celebrate the new invention that was to change the whole role, as well as face, of verse, in verses that appeared in successive works printed by Schoeffer. The words that he chose (several invented by himself, as no current words existed for facts and things so new) are not easy to understand, and his Latin hexameters limp rather than run. But his sense of wonder at the potential of the great new invention, providential in its power to further the word and work of God, is unmistakable.

Besides these panegyrics about the invention itself, he wrote another (and no doubt to him more important) work, a metrical Latin grammar, printed at the press where he worked about *c.* 1455–75. Like Alexander, he was fascinated by exceptions, and his rules abound with lists of words (including some of his own inventions, to which they provide a useful guide). But there his work is, under his own name (suitably obscured in allusive verses). For the first time a poet is confronted with a new and transforming process for his work, its translation into print and through print to a far wider readership than any manuscript could reach. But, primitive as it still was, it was not quite adequate for Borne's work. The sections and conjunctions into which it was divided had to be signalled, and a handful of letters in one size, without the other devices the scribe had at his disposal, were insufficient. So, like the writer of the papyrus with which we began, he dipped his pen in red ink to add the necessary words and point them in the right direction.[57]

When Borne's work came to be reprinted, some two years later, the apparatus of printing had improved: all the added words could now be printed, and only the joining lines had to be added by hand. It is the beginning of a whole new series of compromises between words as they first took form in the poet's head and the words on the printed page that finally convey them to the reader. Most of the words have been copied, either from the author's dictation or some intermediate source. An intervening listener or a scribe was now a diminished factor in the process; other figures – editors, copy-preparers, compositors, publishers – came to fill the gap. The manuscript, however, was not diminished, becoming an alternative to print, as it once was to the voice. But print, its disciplines and artifices, limitations and vast new power to gain and retain readers, now comes to fill the second part of this story. The poet, once rewarded by fame or a patron's purse of gold, begins to take a proprietorial interest in the words that he or she has written, and we a new interest in the form that the poet's pen has given them. What can we read into, or beyond, the words on the sheet of paper that forms a tangible link between us and the writer?

4
The Poet on the Page

There is a paradox in the pattern of survival. If the loss is inevitably greater the further back in time you go, the oldest literature, that of Mesopotamia and Egypt, has only been recovered in relatively recent time. Over five thousand years, innovation and recovery have been constant processes, each intimately connected with the other. Reading and recitation, equally, have been intertwined. Reading verse instantly loses the immediacy of the poet's voice, and reading to one's self, silently and after the event, can only be a lunar reflection of words first spoken or sung. Reading, etymologically, implies reading aloud, and it is important to remember not only that texts were composed and written down to be read aloud over a far longer time than those destined for silent reading, but also that other texts had as long a life or longer before any means of recording them existed at all. By 1500, however, the twin tasks of writing for a live audience and writing to be read had so far coalesced that poetic words now relied on a written record, not only for performance or preservation, but, crucially, as the medium of composition. But even now, ancient habits, the result of seeing as well as hearing verse, persisted, influencing the way poets now wrote down their words, visible signs of a process in the mind's ear of which no record could be kept.

On all these pressures and movements, tradition, closely linked with the *lingua franca* of Latin, exercised a restraining influence. It was only slowly that Latin verse itself came to be written out in the lines – epic, elegiac or lyric – with which we are familiar today. The vastly greater mass of writing in prose, with conventions in terms of punctuation and layout that had nothing to do with verse, influenced the appearance of the minor medium. Masons, too, carving words on stone, naturally tended to fit lines, verse as well as prose, to the generally rectangular tablets on which they worked. The new variety of techniques – alliteration, metre, stress and rhyme – did not bring about new conventions; rather, the need to depict them was expressed by techniques that made them look like prose: line-fillers, brackets joining rhyme lines, initial letters outset from the words to which they belonged.

It is another paradox that printing, due to the limitations of its new technology, could only partially imitate the books of prose or verse that it strove to replicate. Its shortcomings in this respect were liberating. Lacking the scribal apparatus of punctuation, accentuation, ruling, and above all the fluidity and adaptability of script, the printer's compositor did his best to replicate, but where he failed he was forced to innovate, like Johann Borne. If the invention of printing, its technology and business were spread by itinerant Germans, it found its strongest roots in Italy, where coincidentally ways of setting out words on a page were less rigid, less influenced by the example of prose. Experimentation, in letter-forms, format and layout, may have been a necessity, but it was no bar to progress. It is no surprise then that the greatest of post-classical poems should be the first to find its way into print in 1472.

The concept of a rectangular grid, inherited from generations of disciplined scribal book-production, was reinforced by the technology of printing, with its rectangular three-dimensional pages of

Dante *Divina Commedia*,
Foligno, 1472;
Manchester, John Rylands
Library 7295.

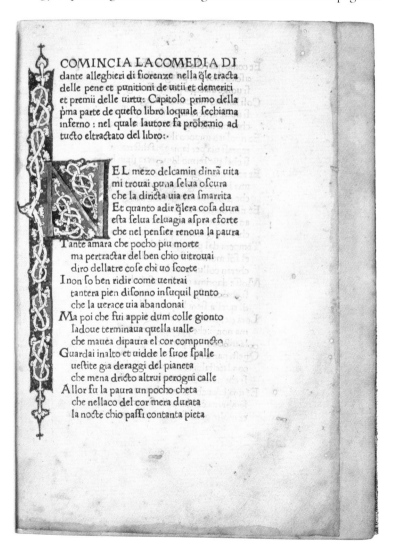

type and binary quire structure. But Dante's *terza rima* had its own asymmetry (three lines, not pairs, arranged in triads), as well as the symmetry that led most scribes to treat each tercet as a stanza, with an outset initial, often in a second colour. Printers, following common manuscript practice which separated the writing of the text from the rubricator's work, habitually allowed space for a *littera notabilior*, into which they set the first letter in the body type, indenting the second and subsequent lines as necessary. Both in manuscript and print, punctuation followed perceived sense, not lineation; the end of the tercet was not automatically pointed.

In the case of Petrarch we have, for the first time, the author's rough drafts as well as his fair copy.[1] It is indescribably moving to see, for the first time, the poet at work, in the very act of changing 'Laura serena che fra verdi fronde / mormorando e per la fronte miemme' to an altogether more vivid 'mormorando a ferir nel volto miemme'. Petrarch had no time for scholastic rules of punctuation, preferring rhetoric, which simply indicated pauses within a sentence, to a grammatical tabulation of different types of structure. In terms of layout, he tended to write two successive verses on a single line, separated by a space of varying size. This conveys a diagonal pattern to the eye in the first two quatrains of the sonnet, while the rhymes of the two tercets fall neatly beneath each other. In the first rough copy, the caesural space varies from wide to non-existent; in the fair copy, it changes from an even space (so that the beginning of the second half of the line is variable) to an uneven space, with the second part of each line aligned. These niceties were lost on the secondary copyists by whom his work was spread abroad. By then a sonnet was a sonnet of 14 lines, written as such. An elegant copy of the 'Canzoniere' made in Venice as early as 1400 has offset initials and no punctuation, as if it were a romance text; another copy made in the Crimea in 1431 is not much different, although the final sestet is marked with an initial red paragraph.[2] The scribes of both books record that they copied Petrarch's *canzoni* while in prison, a reminder that the writing out of verse was not bound to ruling and lineation.

Autograph poetry of any sort of this antiquity is uncommon, but more of it may survive than is recognised as such. All scribes were copyists, in the sense that they followed the conventions just described, whether what they wrote was of their own composing or not. Unless, therefore, a scribe identifies what he writes as his own work, or the hand can be identified as his by comparison with other signed work, an authorial fair copy is not distinguishable from that of any other copyist. There are two manuscripts in the British Library that can be safely claimed as written in their authors' own hands.[3] William Herbert was a Franciscan friar who

Petrarch's 'Canzoniere',
Vat.lat. 3195.

Opposite Petrarch's
'Canzoniere', fair copy,
Vat.lat. 3196.

died at Hereford about 1333.[4] He translated Latin hymns into
English rhyming verse, linking the rhyme words with extended
brackets. The more elaborate *aabccb* scheme is accentuated by
putting the third and sixth lines to the right of the lines that they
follow. He notes his sources, a version of the 'Dies Irae', here,
but distinguishes his own composition by writing his name in
the left margin. Despite the formal appearance of the page, it
bears signs of revision: the last stanza on the page is a revision
of the second of the poem above, carefully marked for insertion
as such. John Shirley, who died in 1456, was in the service of
Richard Beauchamp, the great Earl of Warwick (1382–1439); he
rented four shops in the precincts of St Bartholomew's Hospital,
where he seems to have provided a sort of circulating library,
perhaps for his patron's circle.[5] The books that he wrote and thus
purveyed were anthologies of popular texts, including some by
Chaucer, whom he admired, and Lydgate, whom he knew – the

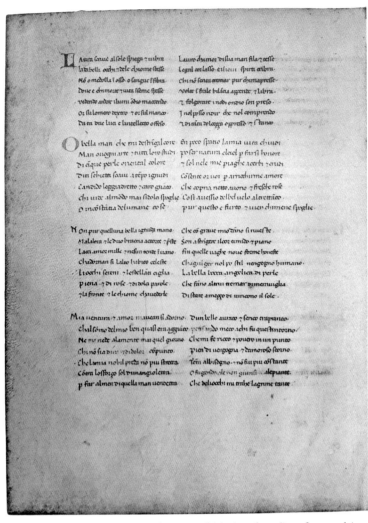

first couplet here (the conclusion of his 'prologe') refers to him.
The rest is directed to his readers:

    And other balades moo ther beon
    Right godely looke, and ye may seen
    And [whane] ye haue this booke ouerlooked
    The right lynes with the crooked
    And the sentence vnderstonden
    With Inne youre mynde hit fast ebounden
    Thanke the thAuctoures that thees storyes
    Renoueld haue to your memoryes
    And the wryter for his distresse
    Whiche besechithe youre gentylesse
    That ye sende this booke ageyne
    Hoome to <u>Shirley</u> that is right feyne
    If hit hathe beon to yowe pleasaunce

As in the Reedyng of the Romaunce
And alle that beon in this companye
God send hem Ioye of hir ladye
And euery womman of hir loue
Prey I to god that sittethe aboue.

The Latin quatrain at the bottom is to the same effect. The paragraph signs that appear to indicate stanzas seem in fact to be arbitrarily placed. The script and layout (on the vellum flyleaves) has an informal appearance, suggestive of a book meant for limited circulation.

Thomas Hoccleve (*c.* 1368–1426) was a more professional scribe, earning his living as a clerk of the Privy Seal, and also a more professional poet. Accustomed to write the chancery or 'secretary' hand, writing *in propria persona* he used a slower, more calligraphic script. This fair copy of his own 'chaunceon', if more elegant both in form and matter (which prefigures Shakespeare's Sonnet 130) than Shirley's, resembles his in layout, though the stanza breaks (a flourished line) are real, and the bracketed lines are followed by the refrain.

The diversity of forms in which poetry could be written down presented printing with a problem, since types were limited in both size and design. 'The Chorle and the Bird' was a simple ballad, one in a collection of different pieces (including 'Octavyan Imperator') preserved in a plain fifteenth-century collection. The Ellesmere copy of the *Canterbury Tales* was written with appropriate splendour. Caxton's response to this was perforce uniform: both ballad and the majestic folio of Chaucer were given the same form, neither English nor French in origin but a version of the calligraphic Burgundian batarde. Perhaps its difference, its unlikeness to letterforms familiar in England, was deliberate, avoiding comparisons that might otherwise have been drawn with all the different manuscript letterforms. But it was, by any standard, a handsome letter, and Caxton may have relied on that alone to carry off its use in such different contexts as the pamphlet 'The Chorle and the Bird' and the folio of the *Canterbury Tales*. His later types were smaller and closer to familiar manuscript forms, but by then the idea, the form of the printed page, was no longer unfamiliar.

John Lydgate, *The Chorle and the Bird*, Westminster, 1477: Cambridge University Library.

Imitating the manuscript book remained a formula for transmitting older poetic texts, older and there-fore reliable in terms of the market. Successive folios of Chaucer in 1532, 1542, 1561, 1598, and even 1602, and Gower's *De Confessione Amantis* (1532, 1554) were all in black-letter, by now the conventional form for rendering such texts.[6] There was a certain irony in this: English types in the later fifteenth century tended to come from France, where *textura* (formal black letter) had been origi-nally the normal letter for Latin texts, while the *batarde* (halfway between formal and current script) was appro-priate for the vernacular. The same phenomenon can be seen in France, the source of English typography. But there the change from the traditional two-column layout in vernacular script, followed by *batarde* type, came earlier. All the pressures that led to the transition from this to a preference for Italianate typography, and roman and italic type, were products of the initial success and subsequent failure of the French invasion of Italy. So, while Villon in print remained firmly 'gothique', the new voice of Clément Marot was firmly 'roman'. The text of the small octavo of 1529 is the same as that of the folio of the previous year, but the barely legible inscription 'Clement Marot m'a donné ce livre' provides confirmation that this edition was the work of the contemporary poet. This may seem surprising, since the manuscript that was used for the later edition, with Marot's 'Préambule', in two columns and in a sort of transitional hand, betrays nothing of the impending typographic change. To compound the problem, Marot himself wrote a vernacular French hand of outstanding beauty.[7]

But this revolution, so apparently sudden (for all that its roots go back to the campaigns in Italy of Charles VIII and Louis XII, and the books of the Aragonese and Sforza libraries that came to France then) and yet far-reaching, in terms of its effect on the transmission of verse in Europe over the next two centuries, is only part of a much larger and longer lasting change in the appearance and structure of books. This change was accelerated, but not initi-

Geoffrey Chaucer, *Canterbury Tales*, Westminster, 1476; Wormsley Library.

ated, by the invention of printing, which however canonised it. Armando Petrucci has shown how the 'modern book', a small (in printing terms octavo) narrow oblong page, evolved from the combination of the university text, the humanistic revival of the classics, and the popular 'vernacular' book designed to be carried in a satchel.[8] The need for simplicity, uniformity and speed in copying of texts for students, the preference of the early Italian humanists for plain unglossed texts of the classics, and the practical concerns of carriage, all led in the same direction. But it was printing, at first imitative and then normative, that came to coordinate these tendencies. To our eye, there is a vast distance between Petrarch's proto-humanistic script and contemporary books of simple vernacular verse, but both elements contributed to the transition, in typographic terms, of verse into its modern form.

Roman de la Rose, Paris, 1528.

Roman de la Rose, Paris, 1529.

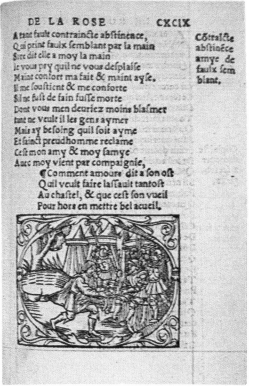

But it was, in fact, prefigured by the most influential of all typo-graphic revolutions to affect poetry, the invention of the Aldine pocket classic. The combination of the small page, exactly the same size as Petrarch's manuscripts (perhaps by no coincidence, its proportions are those of the 'Golden Section'), the use of the new italic type, above all its simplicity, made the series of Aldine classics an instant publishing success. It was much imitated, not only for classical authors, but also for contemporary poets aspiring to classical status, whether they wrote in Latin or the vernac-ular. To be able to write in both was not exceptional, and the sixteenth century was a golden age for the writing of Neo-Latin verse. Poets such as Sannazaro, Vida, Joachim du Bellay, Jean Dorat, George Buchanan and John Owen enjoyed an equal repu-tation with those more famous now for writing in the vernacular. The most successful, in terms of numbers of editions printed, of all sixteenth-century books of poetry was the anthology *Carmina Quinque Poetarum*. But the overlap between Latin and the vernac-ular was total. Villon, if in the *livre de poche* format, looks entirely traditional, without any sign of other influence, classical or Italian; Lodovico Dolci's Italian version of Ovid's classic *Metamorphoses* appeared in the traditional two-column 'romance' format.[9]
Religious reform left its mark on poetry: if *Le Miroir de l'âme*

Horace, *Opera*, Venice, 1501.

Petrarch, *Le Cose Volgari*, Venice, 1501.

LIB . .I.
Neu morem in salium sit requies pedum,
Neu multi damalis meri
Bassum threicia uincat Amystide,
Neu desint epulis rosæ,
Neu uiuax apium,neu breue lilium.
Omnes in Damalim putres
Deponent oculos,nec Damalis nouo
Diuelletur adultero,
Lasciuis ederis ambitiosior.
Ad sodales ob Actiacam Augusti Victoriam
bibendum esse. ODE XXXVII.
Tricolos tetrastrophos.
Nvnc est bibendum,nunc pede libero
Pulsanda tellus,nunc saliaribus
Ornare puluinar deorum
Tempus erat dapibus sodales·
Antehac nefas depromere cæcubum
Cellis auitis,dum capitolio
Regina dementes ruinas,
Funus,et imperio parabat
Contaminato cum grege turpium
Morbo uirorum quodlibet impotens
Sperare,fortunaq; dulci
Ebria,sed minuit furorem
Vix una sospes nauis ab ignibus,
Mentemq; lymphatam marcotico
Redegit in ueros timores
Cæsar ab Italia uolantem
Remis adurgens,accipiter uelut
c ii

Il mio auersario;in cui ueder solete
Gliocchi nostri,ch'amore e'l ciel honora;
Con le non sue bellezze uinnamora
Piu,che'n guisa mortal,soaui et liete·
Per consiglio di lui Donna m'hauete
Scacciato del mio dolce albergo fora,
Misero exilio;auegna ch'io non fora
D'habitar degno,oue uoi sola siete·
Ma s'io u'era con saldi chioui fisso;
Non dueua specchio farui per mio danno
A uoi stessa piacendo aspra et superba·
Certo se ui rimembra di Narcisso;
Questa e quel corso ad un termino uanno:
Benche di si bel fior sia indegna l'herba·

L'oro,et le perle,et fior uermigli e i bianchi;
Che'l uerno deuria far languidi et secchi;
Son per me acerbi et uelenosi stecchi;
Ch'io prouo per lo petto et per li fianchi·
Pero i di miei fien lagrimosi et manchi:
Che gran duol rade uolte auen che'nuecchi·
Ma piu ne'ncolpo i micidiali specchi;
Che'n uagheggiar uoi stessa hauete stanchi·
Quest poser silentio al signor mio,
Che per me ui pregaua;ond'ei si tacque
Veggendo in uoi finir uostro desio:
Quest fer fabbricati sopra l'acque
D'abisso,et tinti nel eterno oblio;
Onde'l principio di mia morte nacque·

pécheresse of Marguerite de Navarre, as printed for her at Alençon, was in batarde, the editions printed in Paris by Antoine Augereau, in which Marot had a hand, moved it firmly into roman type and new orthography. It was Marot, with Théodore de Bèze, who translated the Psalms that came to be the main liturgical resource of Calvin's Geneva. Marot's first Psalms in metre appeared in 1539, but it was the *Pseaumes Octantetrois de David*, first printed at Geneva in 1551 with the tunes of Louis Bourgeois, that canonised them. In 1543 Calvin had written in his preface, 'We will not find better songs, nor more apt to pray and praise God, than the Psalms of David';[10] endemic in the Protestant faith, the English translation of Thomas Sternhold and John Hopkins, begun in 1549, was added to the *Book of Common Prayer* in 1562. *The Psalms in Meeter* became the earliest learned and therefore best known poetry in the English language for over two centuries. Its shortcomings, literary and theological (which occasioned the 'Bay Psalm Book', the first book printed in North America to contain any kind of verse), made no difference to its popularity, and its many forms shaped the way contemporary verse was written and printed.

Illustration was another convention carried over from the Middle Ages and adapted to woodcut form, to augment the words, but without extending already familiar terms of reference. But if *Orlando Furioso* and *Gerusalemme Liberata* continued the tradition of medieval romances, there was one new element: artist and poet might collaborate. Tasso himself had written 'il poeta sia facitor

Les Pseaumes Octantetrois de David, Geneva, 1551.

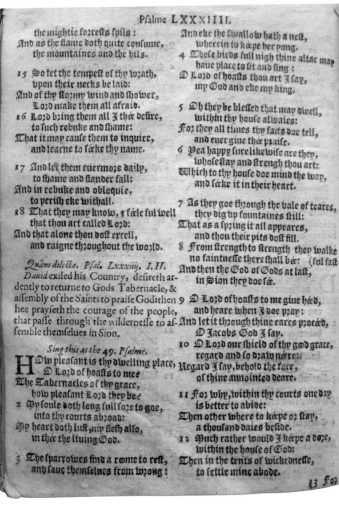

Thomas Sternhold & John Hopkins, *The Whole Book of Psalmes collected into English Meeter*, London, 1617.

degli idoli … ma debbiam dir piu tosto che sia facitore de l'im-
agini a guisa d'un parlante pittore' [the poet may be a maker of
idols, but we should rather say that he makes images like a painter
in speech].[11] He was fortunate enough to find an artist capable of
depicting his spoken images in Bernardo Castello, introduced by
Angelo Grillo with the words 'la penna di Vostra Signoria sia così
spirito del pennello di messer Bernardo, come la sua pittura sarà
corpo de la vostra poesia' [your pen will become the spirit of his
brush as his pictures the body of your poetry].[12] In this he proved
entirely right, and poet and artist hit it off. The engravings that
Agostino Carracci, Giacomo Franco, and later Camillo Cungio
made from Bernardo's work were as influential in later illustration
as Tasso in poetry. Not all poetry was susceptible of illustration,
but there was another entirely novel area, where poetic words and
pictures could combine.

The fashion for emblem books was inaugurated by Andrea
Alciati, whose *Emblemata* appeared for the first time in 1531.

LVI.

QVād le corbeau degloutit le ſerpēt
Au gouſt luy ſēblę vng ſuccrę ou
venaiſon:
Mais puis apres grandemēt ſēn repent,
Car le bō gouſt toſt ſe tournę en poiſon.
Il fault menger & boyre par raiſon,
Et ſoy garder de ſuffoequer nature:
Boirę & manger ſans raiſon ou meſure,
Gaſtę à la fin la ſanté du marchant.
La gueulle faict plus de deſconfiture,
Que ne faict Mars de ſō glaiue trēchāt.

Guillaume de la Perrière, *Théatre des Bons Engins*, Paris, 1539.

The texts were not necessarily poetic, but became a poetic form in their own right, while the combined image-and-texts added both to the matter and form of poetry. Ancient texts, from the fake Egyptian hieroglyphics of Horapollo to the fables of Aesop, fitted as easily into this genre as the texts now specially written by Alciati, Claude Paradin and Guillaume de la Perrière. When Théodore Marcile came to write the introduction to his edition of the *Civitas Veri* of Bartolommeo del Bene in 1609, he pointed to its author's purpose:

Comme il désirait que les lecteurs pussent repaître copieusement leur esprit du suc et de la moelle des théories d'Aristote…, l'auteur a eu recours, pour présenter ce propos, à cette vaisselle qu'est la poésie, et comme celle-ci lui paraissait à peine assez somptueuse pour un tel festin, il l'a accompagnée de sa jumelle, la peinture […]: ce que la plume du poète n'a pas assez bien décrit, le pinceau du peintre le représentera. C'est ce que le poète Simonide a voulu dire par cette formule inspirée: le poème est une peinture douée de parole, la peinture un poème muet. [Desiring that his readers might be able to enjoy the theories of Aristotle, the author has had recourse to the vessel

Sir Thomas Wyatt, 'Tagus fare well…', British Library, Egerton 2711 (Croft 9).

of poetry, and as that seemed hardly sumptuous enough for such a feast, he has accompanied her with her twin, painting […] what the poet's pen has not sufficiently described will be represented by the painter's brush. This is the meaning of the inspired saying of the poet Simonides: the poem is a painting with the gift of speech, the picture a mute poem.][13]

It is against this background that we are to see the first surviving piece of English poetry of which the author's draft and the first printed text both exist. The first part of the manuscript volume of Sir Thomas Wyatt's verse in the British Library[14] was written by a copyist, perhaps engaged to copy his work to date before

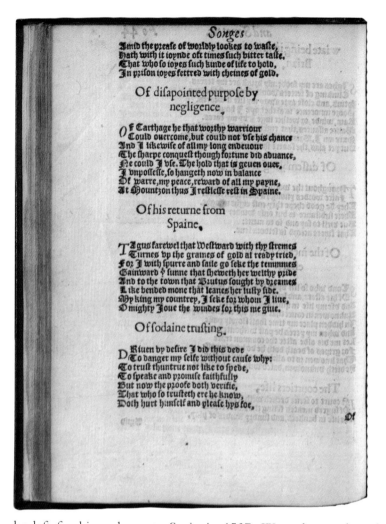

Songes and Sonettes,
London, 1557;
Cambridge, Trinity
College, Cambridge.

he left for his embassy to Spain in 1537. Wyatt later enlarged the book, adding poems in his own hand (a hybrid of English vernacular and humanist italic), some revised as he wrote; these he signed with his 'yt' monogram. Afterwards, another copy was made by a different hand, marking the texts copied as 'ent[ered]'; this may have been part of the process of editing them for publication in 'Tottel's Miscellany', *Songes and Sonettes* (1557). This anthology, which contained the poems of Surrey as well as Wyatt, was responsible for introducing Italian models, in particular the Petrarchan sonnet, to England. The lower poem in the manuscript appeared in it, with the title (perhaps added by the copyist), 'why loue is blinde'. The appearance of *Songes and Sonettes* is also a hybrid, the title-page in italic, the text in black-letter. Although all Wyatt's revisions have been preserved, the text has been altered. Punctuation is added, sometimes wrongly (in other places, words were inserted to fill out the iambic pentameters), and spelling normalised, with initial capitals and 'e' inserted after all Wyatt's terminal 'd's. This suggests two hands, an editor's and (perhaps) a compositor's.

Neither of these can have expected to see their work in print. Wyatt and Surrey were both long dead before their *Songes and Sonettes* came out. The first professional (if print is to be regarded as such a qualification) English poet was Spenser, beginning in 1579 with *The Shepheards Calendar*; sadly, no verse in his hand is known. But Spenser's earliest published work, in *The Theatre for Worldlings* (1568), another anthology of verse already in manuscript circulation, came straight from Italy and France, in imitations of Petrarch and Joachim du Bellay. Mellin de St Gelais, poet laureate to François I, disdained print and his books circulated in elegant calligraphy, only reaching print in 1574, long after his death. By contrast, his younger rival, Ronsard, took naturally to print, and both he and his ally, Joachim du Bellay, author of *La Deffence, et Illustration de la Langue Francoyse* (1549), made full use of the rich resources of the Parisian printers of their time. If Ronsard also knew the value of manuscript (his patron Henri de Mesmes collected his manuscripts,[15] and the dedication copy of 'La Franciade' presented to Charles IX was elegantly written by

Pierre Ronsard, *Les Oeuvres*, Paris, 1584.

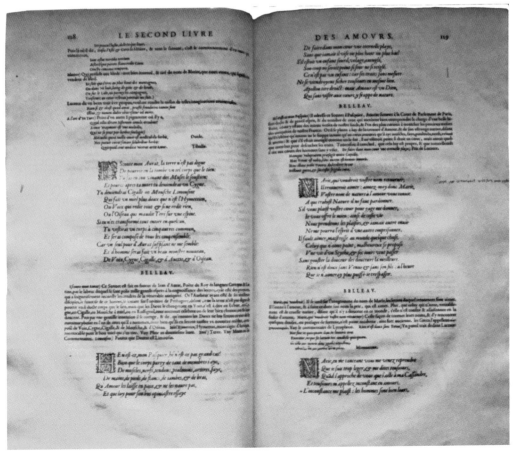

Amadis Jamyn),[16] he was well aware of the promotional value of the press, and was the first poet to command, after five editions in smaller format, a folio edition (1584), with a commentary such as had hitherto been reserved for classical authors.

The dual resources of manuscript and printed circulation took a similar if less luxurious route in England. Too little is known about the scriveners, as opposed to printers, whose work equally fuelled a book trade more diffuse than might be imagined from their several outputs. It is only in recent time that the extent to which different types of text, including poetic texts, circulated in manuscript has begun to emerge.[17] On the other hand, it would be facile to see scriveners as the copy-shops, as opposed to printers proper, of their time. Confidence, given or broken, was an essential part of the equation: a text to be kept private or destined for limited circulation could only be given to a trust-worthy copyist, but, once out of the author's hands, could not be further controlled (though, then as now, it could be deliberately leaked – and authorship denied, if need be). Often, no doubt, these subtleties were beside the point. Authorial property did not exist, as such, and printers' privileges were made to be broken. A poet might make or cause to be made one or more copies, on loose sheets probably (a book was for keeping), but rejoice if others made more, or copied them into a personal 'miscellany' book.[18] Eventually, but it might be a long time later, so much so as to be more often than not posthumous, a collection, more or less authentic, might find its way into print.

The only scrap of Sir Philip Sidney's poetry in his own hand is written at the end of a copy of Bouchet's *Annales d'Aquitaine* (1557). This little lullaby to Desire must have run in his head when he wrote it down, his hand a little cramped by writing in such an awkward place. Two words had changed when, many copies later, it first appeared in print in the third edition of *Arcadia* in 1598. His one point, a comma, comes better after 'Desire'. Sidney's friend, Fulke Greville, Lord Broke, likewise wrote his sonnets without thought of publication, even in manuscript; only his tragedy, *Mustapha*, and one or two poems in miscel-lanies appeared in his lifetime. But he had his 'Caelica' copied by a professional scrivener *c.* 1619, correcting the poems himself (adding a missing couplet left out by the scrivener) in his own extraordinarily illegible hand. Not this manuscript, but one like it, was sent to press by his co-executor, Sir John Coke, to be published in *Certain Learned and Elegant Workes* in 1633, five years after Greville's death. It incorporates the changes that he made (his own odd spelling 'checquere' becomes 'Exchequer'), but otherwise it follows copy scrupulously, even in punctuation and the large initial with which each sonnet begins.

ennemis au sainct siege Apostolic, mesmement en aiant esté supplié de ce faire.
¶ *S'il a defendu comme Vicaire du sainct Empire les Allemagnes contre l'opresse de l'Empereur, il a maintenant beaucoup meilleure, cause comme filz de defendre noftre sainct Pere, & auroit (otées toutes les autres iniures) cette cy feule, asses d'argument pour rompre la Trefue, mais les aduersaires premiers par leurs pratic— ges l'ont enfrainte,*

FIN.

Sir Philip Sidney 'Sleep Baby...'; Cologny, Geneva, Bibliotheca Bodmeriana (Croft 14).

That here is iufter caufe of plaintful fadneffe,
Thine earth now fprings, mine fadeth: (deth.
Thy thorne without, my thorne my heart inua-

To the tune of Bafciami vita mia.

SLeep Babie mine, Defire nurfe beauty fingeth:
Thy cryes, O Babie, fet mine head on aking:
The Babe cries way, thy loue doth keep me wa-
(king.

Lully, Lully, my Babe, hope cradle bringeth
Vnto my children alway good reft taking:
The Babe cries way, thy loue doth keep me waking.

Since baby mine, from me thy watching fpringeth,
Sleep then a little, pap content is making:
The babe cries nay for that abide I waking.

To the tune of the fpanifh fong, Se tu fennora
no dueles de mi.

OFaire, O fweet, when I do look on thee,
In whom all ioyes fo well agree,
Heart and foule do fing in me.
This you heare is not my tongue,
VVhich once faid what I conceaued,
For it was of vfe bereaued,
With a cruell anfwer flong.
No, though tongue to roofe be cleaued,
Fearing leaft he chaftifde be,
Heart and foule do fing in me.

Sidney, *Arcadia*, London, 1598.

Sir John Harington's translation of Ariosto illustrates many more stages in this process. Apart from some early draft sheets,[19] what is the earlier of two surviving manuscripts,[20] both incomplete, is already a fair copy, of which Harington wrote the first stanza and a scrivener the rest. The other[21] is the autograph, with punctuation added, probably by Harington, that was used by Richard Field as setting copy (with the cast-off marked) for the first edition of 1591. This was probably printed for the author, certainly under

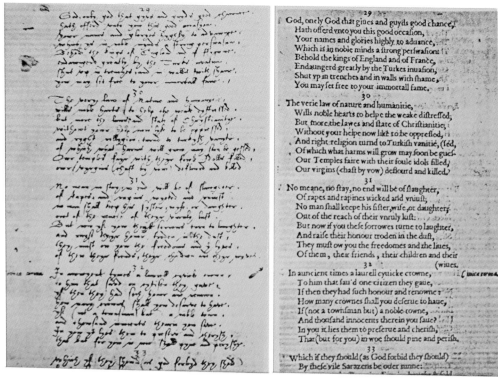

29

God, onely God that giues and guyds good chance,
Hath offerd vnto you this good occasion,
Your names and glories highly to aduance,
Which is in noble minds a strong perswasion
Behold the kings of England and of France,
Endaungerd greatly by the Turkes inuasion,
Shut vp in trenches and in walls with shame,
You may set free to your immortall fame.

30

The verie law of nature and humanitie,
Wills noble hearts to helpe the weake distressed;
But more the lawes and state of Christianitie,
Without your helpe now likt to be oppressed,
And right religion turnd to Turkish vanitie, (sed,
Of which what harms will grow may soon be gues-
Our Temples faire with their foule idols filled,
Our virgins (chast by vow) deflourd and killed.

31

No meane, no stay, no end will be of slaughter,
Of rapes and rapines wicked and vniust,
No man shall keepe his sister, wife, or daughter,
Out of the reach of their vnruly lust:
But now if you these sorrowes turne to laughter,
And raise their honour troden in the dust,
They must ow you the freedomes and the liues,
Of them, their friends, their children and their
(wiues.
In auncient times a laurell cyuicke crowne, (nice reward.
To him that sau'd one citizen they gaue,
If then they had such honour and renowne?
How many crownes shall you deserue to haue,
If (not a townsman but) a noble towne,
And thousand innocents therein you saue?
In you it lies them to preserue and cherish,
That (but for you) in woe should pine and perish.

33

Which if they should (as God forbid they should)
By these vile Sarazens be oder runne:

Sir John Harington's Ariosto, *Orlando Furioso*, manuscript, British Library, Add.18920, and in print, London, 1591 (P. Gaskell, *Writer to Reader*, pp. 18–21).

his eye. Two more 'commercial' editions followed in 1607, with some authorial corrections, and in 1634, made unaltered from 1607. Extracts appear in at least eight manuscript miscellanies over the same period.[22] Comprehension of this process was inhibited until recently by the assumption that Harington's hand and his copyist's were the same (and therefore both autograph). The copyist's spelling is however more modern ('you' and 'if' in place of 'yow' and 'yf') than Harington's, although his copy is virtually unpunctuated, as Harington's own fair copy may have been originally. Setting this in roman type, Field modernised the spelling, and normalised the punctuation, substituting semi-colons and colons for some of Harington's commas at the end of lines. The process of tidying up continued when 'secondly imprinted' in 1607.

William Drummond of Hawthornden stands apart from his contemporaries, as a Scotsman, a cosmopolitan traveller, the friend of Drayton and Jonson, the owner of a large library; a substantial part of his papers still exists, now in the National Library of Scotland, written in his rugged, upright, characteristically Scottish hand (note the barred 'u').[23] Especially interesting, from our point of view, he wrote for print: his lament for Prince Henry, *Teares on the Death of Meliades*, was printed by Andrew Hart and published in Edinburgh in 1613, and reprinted the following year. Probably, then, he had Hart print his *Poems* for private circulation; a second

Opposite William Drummond, National Library of Scotland 2062, f7a (Croft 29), and in *Poems*, Edinburgh, 1614 and 1616.

edition was published in 1616. His sonnets commemorate Mary Cunningham, who died on the eve of their wedding. The manuscript here starts off as fair copy, but the final couplet changes meaning as well as shape at least twice. The printer's copy must have had further changes: 'secret grief' has become 'inward Woes', and what started as 'wailing' before altered to 'direful' ended back as 'wailing'. Spelling faithfully follows Drummond's, but not the capitalisation; punctuation is added. When the published edition of *Poems* was set in 1616 in the same fount, the compositor spaced out the words, which makes the page look quite different. Not only the text ('Let it suffice' for 'May 't not suffice', 'calme secret Shades' for 'sweet silent Groves'), but the spelling and punctuation have also changed in a way that must be authorial. The use of parentheses (*lunulae*) to surround the conditional clause in the penultimate line, and the query with which it ends, must also be authorial.[24]

SON.

MY Teares may well *Numidian* Lions tame,
And Pitie breed into the hardest Hart
That euer PYRRHA did to Maide impart,
When She them first of blushing Rockes did frame.
Ah Eyes which only serue to waile my smart,
How long will you my inward Woes proclaime,
May't not suffice you beare a weeping Part
All Night, at day but you must doe the same?
Cease idle Sighes to spend your Stormes in vaine,
And these sweet silent Groues for to molest,
Containe you in the Prison of my Brest,
You doe not ease but agrauate my Paine,
    Or if burst forth you must, that Tempest moue
    In Sight of her whome I so dearely loue.

SON.

YOu restlesse Seas apeace your roaring Waues,
And you who raise huge Mountaines in that Plaine
Aires Trumpetters, your hideous Sounds containe,
And listen to the Plaints my Griefe doth cause.
Eternall *Lights*, though adamantine Lawes
Of Destinies to moue still you ordaine,
Turne hither all your Eyes, your Axeltre pause,
And wonder at the Torments I sustaine.
Sad Earth if thou made dull by my Disgrace
Be not, and senselesse, aske those Powers aboue
Why they so crost a Wretch brought on thy Face,
Fram'd for Mishap, th'*Anachorit* of Loue,
    And bid them if they would moe ÆTNAS burne,
    In RHODOPE or ERIMANTHE me turne.

20b

THE FIRST PART.

Son.

MY Teares may well *Numidian* Lions tame,
And Pitie breede into the hardest Hart
That euer *Pirrha* did to Maide impart,
When Shee them first of blushing Rockes did frame.
Ah Eyes which only serue to waile my Smart,
How long will you mine inward Woes proclaime?
Let it suffice you beare a weeping Part
All Night, at Day though yee doe not the same:
Cease idle Sighes to spend your Stormes in vaine,
And these calme secret Shades more to molest,
Containe you in the Prison of my Brest,
You not doe ease but aggrauate my Paine,
    Or (if burst foorth you must?) that Tempest moue
    In Sight of Her whome I so dearely loue.

Son.

NYmphes, Sister *Nymphes* which haunt this christall Brooke,
And (happie) in these Floting Bowrs abide,
Where trembling Rooues of Trees from Sunne you hide,
Which make *Ideall Woods* in euery Crooke,
Whether yee Garlands for your Lockes prouide,
Or pearlie Letters seeke in sandie Booke,
Or count your Loues when *Thetis* was a Bride?
Lift vp your golden Heads and on mee looke.
Read in mine Eyes mine agonizing Cares,
And what yee read recount to Her againe:
Faire Nymphes, say all these Streames are but my Teares,
And if Shee aske you how they sweet remaine,
    Tell that the bitrest Teares which Eyes can powre,
    When shed for Her doe cease more to be sowre. *Like*

John Donne, 'Letter to Lady Carew', Oxford, Bodleian Library, Eng. Poet. d. 197, and (*opposite*) in *Poems*, London, 1633.

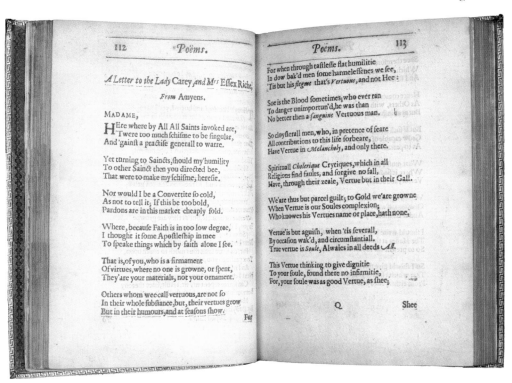

Why did Drummond take such an interest in the press, while his English contemporaries kept it at arm's length? Surely because in Edinburgh, unlike London, there was no regular corps of scriveners through whom gradual circulation, through ever widening concentric circles of readers, might be accomplished. It was Hart who provided the copies, first for a few, then for more readers.

The only unusual feature of this process is that which strikes us as normal, namely the intervention of the author's hand and intention in the passage of his work through the press. The case of Donne is very different. Although the idea of printing his verses was under discussion in December 1614, his ordination next month seems to have put paid to the plan, and they were not printed until 1633, after his death. Manuscript circulation was another matter. There are more copies of Donne's poems in miscellanies and elsewhere than of any other contemporary author: over 4000 instances are known, and there are over 60 miscellanies with substantial collections, none exactly datable, but some representing groups that must have already existed in some form as early as 1590. None of the manuscripts can be identified as copy for the first edition in print, although it is clearly based on one like those in wide circulation in the 1620s and 30s. These continued to be made after the printed editions of 1635, 1639 and probably even after the seventh edtion in 1669 – the two circulation systems continued, independent but not unaware of each other. No autograph of any Donne poem was known until 1970, when the fair copy of his verse epistle to Lady Carew was identified by Peter Croft among the papers of the Duke of Manchester.[25] This is the actual letter sent by Donne from France and addressed by him 'To the Honorable lady the lady Carew'. The poem appears in nineteen miscellanies,[26] variously titled. Printed in 1633, it was 'A Letter to the Lady Carey, and Mrs Essex Riche, From Amyens'.

Strictly speaking, no comparison can exist here between manuscript and print, since an immeasurable gulf of intervening copies lies between them. But the contrast is striking: between the fine white Genoa paper, gilt-edged, of the actual missive, and the rough off-white of the printer's stock; between Donne's individual and (in its way) handsome script and the rough-hewn typography; and, after all, between the texts. That Donne's more idiosyncratic spellings, 'y' for 'i', terminal 'ee' for 'y' or 'ie', for example, should be normalised is not surprising. Other differences – such as 'who is' for 'who are a firmament' – may be due to some pedantic intervening scribe. The omission of the comma between the two 'All's in the first line, destroying the antithesis between vulgar humanity and the saints, is probably the compositor's error; as we have seen, this tended to concentrate on the ends of lines. Donne's own capitalisation and punctuation, his marks of elision (even when the letter elided is written), and the emphatic double letters, are calculated – echoes, like Robert Bridges's orthographic experiments, of spoken emphases. Some but not all of this survives in print: the capitalisation veers towards nouns only, and the italics introduce a new and inauthentic variation: 'Alwaies in all deeds *All*' destroys the impact of three equal 'all's. Donne was willing his sheet to speak; all sound has gone from the printed page.

5
The Muse in Print

So far from subordinating, still less extinguishing, manuscript as the primary means of recording verse, the printed page was, two centuries after its invention, still a secondary, or at best a parallel, means of preserving and divulgating poetry. If memory was the poet's first necessity, paper and a pen for drafting were as necessary. If poetry in progress, like Milton's draft of *Comus*, rarely survives this early, the spread of its texts can now be traced, by oral as well as literal transmission, by writing, from the ornamental dedication manuscript to the travels of a single poem from miscellany to miscellany, as much as or more than in print. The little notebook in which Sir Daniel Fleming, High Sheriff of Westmoreland and a notable book-collector, put down extracts from his reading and other memoranda illustrates this point. Nor were the two modes of diffusion opposed to each other: each served the other and both were served by the same 'trade', scriveners, printers, book-sellers and stationers, who traditionally made a living out of the market for words in any form. One of them supplied this little blank book for Sir Daniel Fleming to use.

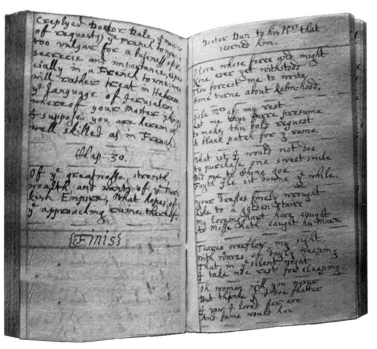

Sir Daniel Fleming's notebook.

Ben Jonson, *Works*, 1616, pp.453–4.

It is only the folly of later scholarship that has divided manuscripts from printed books, notionally (a more venial error or, unforgivably, by physical section. Many a book originally containing verse pieces in both manuscript and print has thus been split up, destroying evidence of authorship, ownership and readership, simply to segregate manuscript and print. Printed books imperfect due to unequal press-runs of individual sheets were often made up in contemporary manuscript. Such books are now sadly rare, since the modern passion for completion saw them only as quarries from which to make up from two or three such a single 'perfect' (but sophisticated) copy. The manuscript leaves were jettisoned, and with them evidence, perhaps even textual evidence, that cannot be replaced.

A combination of factors, notably an increase in demand but also in government control, led to change. Poetry passed into wider circulation; it owed less to word of mouth, and was more often made to be read, and, more and more, read in a portable form. There is a significant growth in the production of scriveners' copies of verse miscellanies, made to order, perhaps even speculatively, in the 1620s and 1630s. The impulse for this came from the market, now grown beyond a circle in which individual pieces might circulate in sheet form. The Star-Chamber *Decree* in 1637 and its relaxation in 1641 had a noticeable impact, as did the inhibition of movement during the Civil War. If Donne first appeared in quarto and Greville in folio, both books were retrospective. Younger poets, or those who saw their work to and through the press, looked to publication in octavo or smaller format. Economy in the cost of publication was not a negligible factor. A book that could travel in a pocket was an asset in troubled times (it was World War II that made paperbacks universally popular). For all these reasons, poets and printers and booksellers drew closer together. One book, in particular, exercised an influence out of all proportion to its size.

None of the foregoing poets, the transmission of whose works we have so far considered, wrote with any apparent thought for the needs of future printing, still less for its visual demands. It is hard not to believe that the manuscript of George Herbert's poetry in Dr Williams's Library[1] was written with this eventuality in mind, since it is so like the printed page of *The Temple* (1633). But which came first? The enormous success of *The Temple* (fifteen editions to 1709) made it the model for many other small books of verse, so it may be that the 'little book' that Herbert sent to Nicholas Ferrar three weeks before his death, to be quickly printed as *The Temple*, was indeed the prime model. The community founded by the Ferrar brothers at Little Gidding had strong and clear views on the importance of the form in which to present God's Word (of which Herbert

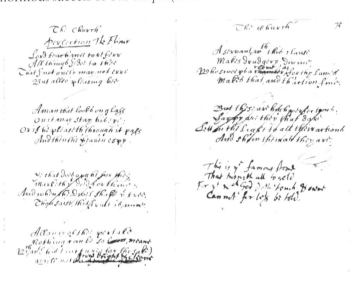

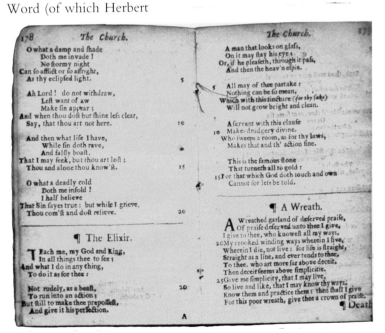

George Herbert's 'The Elixir': Dr Williams's Library, MS. Jones B 62, ff.74v–5 (Croft 34) and *The Temple*, Cambridge, 1633.

said 'he would not part with one leaf thereof for the whole world, if it were offered him in exchange'). But this manuscript is not the 'little book': it is not in Herbert's hand, but here, as elsewhere, it presents early versions that Herbert worked over. Two verses were already complete and perfect, apart from 'roome as' for 'chamber', but the fourth verse is transformed by its revision ('grow bright and cleane' is written over a feebler 'to Heaven grow'), and the first and second printed verses are still to emerge from the discarded manuscript verses 1, 3 and 5. The last verse is all in Herbert's hand; the printed text follows it precisely, apart from the added colon. But even the punctuation is not far from Herbert's: Ferrar was evidently a scrupulous editor. The most interesting variant is the italic, as well as *lunulae*, for the magic word 'tincture'. This can be paralleled exactly in Marlowe's *Hero and Leander* for the invitation that Hero let slip, 'a precise graphic registration of […] unwittingness of speech'.[2]

The fine italic hand of Thomas Carew in 'To Ben Johnson' can have presented few problems to the compositor of his *Poems* (1640).[3] The one change in the manuscript ('age' for 'world') is emphasised with a capital in print. There are few other changes, the compositor even less disposed to change the poet's 'exact and expressive punctuation'. The three parentheses created in print are interesting: each represents a contrasted thought, ranging from a single epithet to a clause, in apposition to the main drift of the argument.[4] These are remote compositorial conventions and must represent authorial intervention, though Carew died just before his book came out.

James Shirley, 'A Curse', Oxford, Bodleian Library, Rawl. Poet.88, ff. 77–8 (Croft 40), and in print, *Poems*, London, 1646.

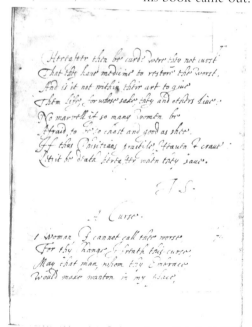

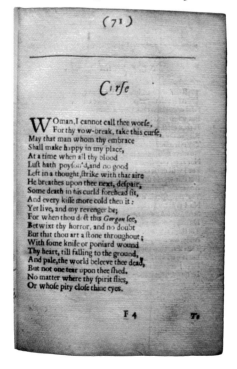

James Shirley wrote an even more elegant hand than Carew, with which he wrote the last two pages of an otherwise scribal collection of his poems.[5] This is remote from the printed *Poems* (1646) in both content and text. Although the first four lines of 'A Curse' resemble each other in both manuscript and print, the rest diverges, as if Shirley had lost the sheet from which he copied the second page of the manuscript and had to finish off the poem as printed quite differently, with only echoes of the earlier text. It is another example of the different paths that poetry could take simultaneously in manuscript and print, for all that Shirley was an experienced and already printed author.

Thomas Randolph's 'On Six Maids' circulated, predictably enough, in manuscript, appearing in print for the first time in the second edition of his poems (1640). This fair copy on a loose sheet shows that the poet enjoyed writing in his wild way, and played tricks with it that defied the compositor. The one change he made ('these' for 'that') shows that his mind had strayed as he wrote ('that' would have made nonsense of the next line), or else that he misread 'what', as preserved in print. The differences in the latter suggest that it was based on a copy that contained both authorial and non-authorial variants. Randolph's punctuation is erratic, and the syntax of the second paragraph ('A

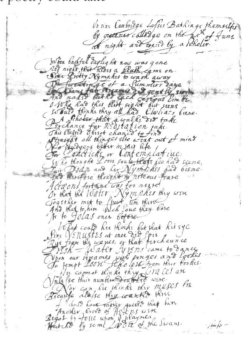

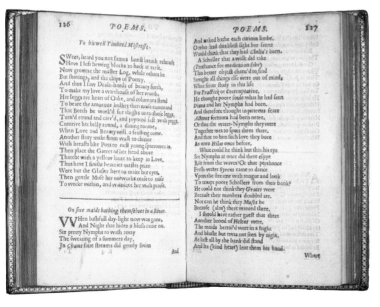

Thomas Randolph, 'On Six Cambridge Lasses...', Oxford, Worcester College MS 346 (Croft 43), and in *Poems*, London, 1668.

Scholer that a walke did take…'), which goes with a swing barely disturbed by an irrelevant comma and point, is made no better by being tidied up in print. The witty emphases created by the words written large are quite lost in print, where they are erratically rendered by initial capitals or italic. The parentheses in *lunulae* are all ironic asides, both in manuscript and print, and must be authorial, for all that there is no correspondence in the two versions. This was a trick that Marvell deployed with greater subtlety.[6]

Milton's *Comus* is remarkable for the number of witnesses with potential authority that exist: his own draft worked on over years, the Bridgewater manuscript presented about the time of the first performance (1634), the first printed text produced by the composer Henry Lawes, without Milton's name but with his further corrections (1637), the first acknowledged printing in *Poems* (1645) and the last lifetime edition in *Poems* (1673). As its appearance suggests, the Bridgewater manuscript was written by a scrivener with an old-fashioned taste in spelling and punctuation. That it was his, not Milton's, is shown by the relatively consistent nature of the others, at least as far as the words are concerned. The variety of spelling suggests that Milton was not greatly interested in it; his own light punctuation is pretty faithfully reproduced in 1637, while 1645 and 1673 (set from 1645) offer the denser punctuation noticed before, more likely therefore to be compositorial. In terms of appearance, it is clear that Lawes took a good deal of trouble with his book in 1637; while the compositors in 1645 and 1673, following lightly corrected printed copy, were less careful. Nor did Milton mind, apparently, feeling perhaps with reason that the words spoke for themselves.[7]

Dryden's flattering 'Heroique Stanza's, Consecrated to the Glorious Memory of his most Serene and Renowned Highnesse' exists in fair copy,[8] and also in print as one of the *Three Poems Upon the Death of his Late Highnesse Oliver, Lord Protector* (1659). Dryden's copy, perhaps made to circulate among friends before publication, is in his neat italic, with secretary 'e', the last such form to survive erosion by the now universal copper-plate (a tribute to the ubiquitous Edward Cocker). Its sobriety contrasts forcibly with the elaborate typography. It is not the copy sent to the printer (at least, it bears no signs of printing-house use), but that must have been virtually identical. Even Dryden's spelling is followed, apart from 'authentick… choice' for 'authentique… choise'; the afterthought 'Least' for 'Lest' is also missed. Where the printed pointing differs it is predictably conventional, and sometimes, as in omitting the comma after 'Romans', plainly wrong. The few italicisations are not conventional and echo Dryden's emphases, as in the capitalised 'Eager'; they may be authorial. But the striking difference lies in the heading; the emphatic large type, its variety

Opposite Abraham Cowley, 'Pindaique Ode', Oxford, Bodleian Library, C 2.21 Art (Croft 51), and in *Poems,* 1656 and 1663.

and the ornamental headpiece and initial, may have been called for by the occasion, but they are an early sign of a new change.

When Cowley presented a large-paper copy of his *Poems* (1656) to the Bodleian Library at Oxford, he added a special 'Pindarique Ode' to the University Library in his own fair copy.[9] This was subsequently printed in his little *Verses, Lately Written upon Several Occasions* (1663), published by Henry Herringman. Here, by contrast, the manuscript is infinitely more imposing than the print. His hand, more florid but as elegant as Dryden's, employs every device — spacing, swash capitals and variation of size — to create an impression worthy of a different occasion. The printed text is, apart from the conventional drop initial, unemphatic, and not only in the heading. The exclamation marks are cut down, and the supporting commas after each 'Hail' are all gone. The spelling is conventional, and the re-punctuation must be by the same hand,

ODE.

Mr. Cowley's *Book presenting it selfe to the University Library of* Oxford.

Hail Learnings *Pantheon* ! Hail the sacred Ark
Where all the World of Science do's imbarque !
Which ever shall withstand, and hast so long withstood,
    Insatiate Times devouring Flood.
Hail Tree of Knowledg, thy leaves Fruit ! which well
Doft in the midft of Paradise arise,
    Oxford the Mufes Paradife,
From which may never Sword the bleft expell.
Hail Bank of all paft Ages ! where they lye
T' inrich with intereft Posterity !
    Hail VVits Illuftrious Galaxy !
VVhere thoufand Lights into one brightnefs fpread;
Hail living University of the Dead !

2.

Unconfus'd Babel of all tongues which er' e   (veles
The mighty Linguift Fame, or Time the mighty Tra
    That could fpeak, or this could hear.
Majeftick Monument and Pyramide,
VVhere ftill the fhapes of parted Souls abide '
Embalm'd in verfe, exalted fo us which now
Enjoy thofe Arts they wou'd fo well below,
    VVhich now all wonders plainly fee,
    That have been, are, or are to be,

In the myfterious Library,
The Beatifick *Bodley* of the Deity.

3.

VVill you into your Sacred throng admit
    The meaneft Brittifh VVit ?
You Gen'ral Council of the Priefts of Fame,
    VVill you not murmur and difdain,
    That I place among you claim,
    The humbleft Deacon of her train ?
VVill you allow me th'honourable chain ?
    The chain of Ornament which here
    Your noble Prifoner proudly wear ;
A Chain which will more pleafant feem to me
Than all my own Pindarick Liberty :
VVill ye to bind me with thofe mighty names fubmit,
    Like an Apocrypha with holy VVrit ?
VVhat ever happy book is chained here,
Nor other place or People need to fear ;
His Chain's a Pafport to go ev'ry where.

4.

    As when a feat in Heaven,
Is to an unmalicious Sinner given,
    VVho cafting round his wondring eye,
Does none but Patriarchs and Apoftles there efpye ;
    Martyrs who did their lives beftow,
    And Saints who Martyrs liv'd below ;
VVith trembling and amazement he begins,
To recollect his frailties paft and fins,

B   H3

since it inserts a futile new exclamation after 'Bank of all past Ages', compounding it with an equally pointless semi-colon at the end of the next line. Cowley does not seem to have minded these intrusions any more than Milton, and the text was reprinted without change, clearly from the printed copy of 1663 in the first edition of his *Works* (1668) and the many subsequent editions, all also published by Herringman.

Cowley's ever popular *Works* were printed in folio. *The Workes of Benjamin Jonson*, proudly so titled in 1616, had been a landmark in English publishing, the works of a modern author for the first time given a classical frame. It was not the first poetic folio, for *Poly-Olbion* had been printed in folio in 1612. Its real model was the 1584 *Oeuvres* of Ronsard, the culmination of a long and well-judged campaign to promote his work. Fifty years later, François de Malherbe could indite a sonnet to the Dauphin in a manuscript that differs little from that which Ronsard presented to Charles IX; the printed text that followed was set in the same italic types first cut almost a century earlier. Another fifty years later, the model remained still unchanged in Boileau's influential 'Art Poétique', first published in 1674. If there were signs of change, it was not so much in the vernacular as in Latin, notably in the famous hymns and poems in Latin verse of Jean-Baptiste de Santeuil, constantly reprinted. Hymnody, from the Geneva psalms to the Wesleys, is a

Torquato Tasso,
Gerusalemme Conquistata,
manuscript, Naples,
Biblioteca Nazionale, and
in print, Rome, 1593.

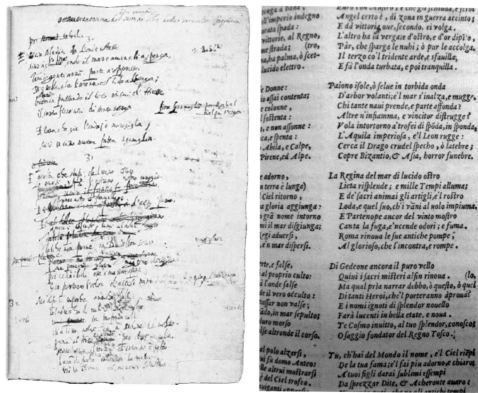

constant undercurrent in secular verse. Herbert was preserved in the Moravian hymn-book,[10] and Sir H.W. Baker, author of 'The King of Love my Shepherd is', translated Santeuil for *Hymns Ancient and Modern*.[11]

But of all the models that influenced poetic ideas and diction, as well as their form, in the seventeenth century and later, the greatest and most pervasive was Tasso. If *Gerusalemme Liberata* was the most famous, *Aminta*, *Rinaldo* and *Il Re Torrismondo* were hardly less popular in their time. This enormous popularity made his works a canonical model, and spread with a rapidity that exceeded all previous literary best-sellers. This is the more remarkable since the author had little part in the passage of his work into printed form. He had been imprisoned from 1579, so it was almost inevitable that *Gerusalemme Liberata*, already circulating in manuscript, should be pirated when it reached print. The first such edition, incomplete, appeared in Venice in 1580; two rival complete editions, each with a different 'editor', came out

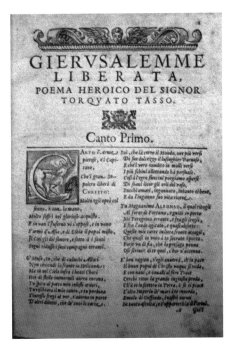

Torquato Tasso, *Gerusalemme Liberata*, Casalmaggiore, 1581, and Genoa, 1617.

next year at Parma and Casalmaggiore, followed, still in 1581, by the Ferrara edition, which has a real claim to authenticity. No manuscript of the *Gerusalemme Liberata* is known, but that of its sequel, *Gerusalemme Conquistata*, survives entire. Tasso, who could write a beautiful hand in fair copy, composed with a speed far beyond his hand's capacity to keep up. The printed text is clearly set from a cleaner subsequent copy, although it follows what little punctuation Tasso supplied with surprising accuracy, as well as supplementing it, sometimes unnecessarily. The first edition, printed at Rome in 1593, was also produced at speed, with the author's intervention in proof; this resulted in a long but by no means comprehensive list of errata.[12]

Despite the splendour and beauty of the illustrations that quickly accompanied the Italian epics, the 1584 Ariosto and the 1590 Genoa Tasso were only in quarto; the first folio *Gerusalemme Liberata* was printed, again at Genoa, in 1617. Real splendour in verse was reserved in the first place for the classics, a notable feature of the publishing programme of the Imprimerie Royale, founded by Cardinal Richelieu in 1640. Ecclesiastical as well as national rivalry, however, was responsible for the equally impressive appearance bestowed on the contemporary verse of popes. Urban VIII's popular sacred Latin verse, reprinted as late as 1726 at Oxford, was published in rival editions by the Typographia Vaticana (1628) and the newly founded Jesuit press in Rome (1631), the latter determined to outdo the former.

These models were not reserved exclusively for the classics, or at least poetry in the classical languages. John Ogilby was essentially a graphic entrepreneur, who saw in the new optimism of the Commonwealth a new market for classical verse (with his own translation for those not so well up in Latin) in grand folio with engraved plates, after fashionable Dutch artists, Francis Clein and Abraham van Diepenbeck. Ogilby financed his works by subscription, a new method of bookselling, like advertising, that evolved during the Civil War, when ordinary lines of trade communication were interrupted. Virgil, Homer and Aesop (twice) were given this treatment, remarkable in England, if imitated from the similar illustrated classics of Michel de Marolles in France (as they were from those of the Imprimerie Royale). The experiment was clearly a success: although Ogilby lost much stock in the Great Fire in 1666 and was forced to hold a lottery of salvaged books to recoup his losses, his books are not rare today. The money that he made went into equally inventive map-publishing; he had a Midas touch. But in artistic terms, Ogilby could not touch the rival Aesop of Francis Barlow, who etched his own plates. These include the English verse texts of John Philipott; Robert Codrington supplied the Latin version below and the

French facing it. Barlow may have intended his book to sell, like modern *livres de peintre*, to an international market, but it seems to have been absorbed locally; a number of copies were bound with great elegance by an anonymous craftsman known as 'the Barlow's Aesop Binder'.[13] What was fit for the classics was no less fit for the great English epic, and the folio *Paradise Lost* (1688) was decorated with striking plates of baroque imagery after the designs of Sir John Baptist Medina.

If one kind of poetry could be given greater prominence and elegance by size alone, pressure in a similar direction came from an entirely different quarter. War – the Thirty Years' War, the

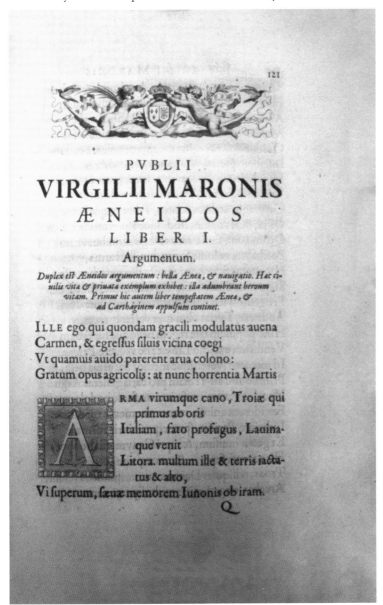

Vergil, *Works*, translated by John Ogilby, London, 1654.

Fronde, the English Civil War – put a new and entirely different value on news. Hitherto, it had been collected and presented in manuscript form by those – spies or political agents – who sold it, with varying degrees of secrecy, to great men, rulers and their civil servants, who needed it. The same band of professional writers who were also capable of writing verse miscellanies gave news as much circulation as was politically permissible. Newsletters appeared in print about 1620, and printed news, in troubled times, spread like wildfire. The quarto sheets that the newsletter-writers sent to their masters were converted into folio sheets, and folio thus became the format of the highly topical verse in which current events were commented on. Innocent affairs, the births, deaths and marriages of important personages, were thus celebrated; the same format was used for political squibs and satires, altogether more dangerous.

The Restoration in Britain might have brought peace, but it did not suppress the spirit of independence of thought that had characterised the two previous decades. Thomas, Earl of Danby, Lord High Treasurer from 1674, was impeached for conducting secret negotiations with France in March 1679 and sent to the Tower. The republican Henry Neville, translator of Machiavelli, sharply pointed the moral of his fall. The title page is set out like a poster (which it no doubt also was), in which the largest and most striking word is 'POEM'. The large well-spaced text type

Henry Neville, *The Sentiments*, London, 1679.

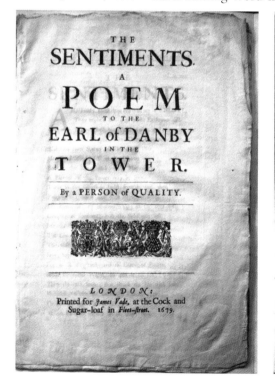

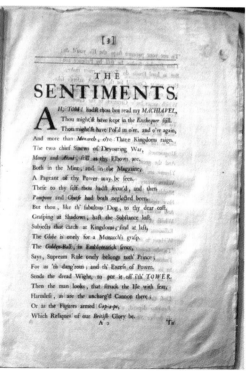

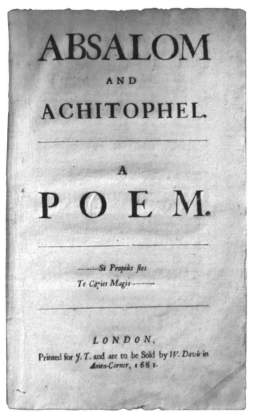
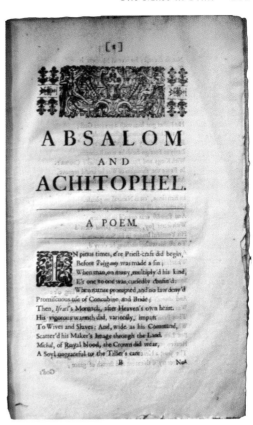

John Dryden, *Absalom and Achitophel*, London, 1681.

('Who runs may read') is as eye-catching. There is no specimen of Neville's hand, but I suspect his copy was hastily written, with phonetic elisions and little punctuation, the latter supplied too generously by the compositor with the usual preference for marks at the ends of lines – one too many, six up from the foot.

'Yet if a *Poem* have a *Genius*, it will force its own reception in the World. For there's a sweetness in good Verse, which Tickles even while it Hurts.' *Absalom and Achitophel* was Dryden's onslaught on the Whigs over the Exclusion Act, but he rightly saw that translating the machinations of Shaftesbury and the Duke of Monmouth into the biblical world counted for less than the point and magic of poetry. Note again the prominence of 'POEM', and the opening lines, as striking as his elegy for Cromwell; on the example of that, it seems likely that if the capitals are perhaps Dryden's, the italics and punctuation, both conventional, are not. No one was more incensed by Dryden's satire than its chief butt as Zimri, the Duke of Buckingham,

A man so various that he seemed to be
Not one, but all mankind's epitome.
Stiff in opinions, always in the wrong;
Was everything by starts, and nothing long:

But, in the course of one revolving moon,
Was chemist, fiddler, statesman and buffoon.

Whether or no he wrote *Poetical Reflections on a late Poem*, published next year, it was clearly inspired by him, and, if Dryden saw long-term fame in medium rather than message, Buckingham was as outraged by his abuse of it. 'If anything, call'd a *Poem*, deserv'd a severe Reflection', it is this 'scandalous Phamphlet [a fine misprint] (unworthy the denomination of *Poesy*) no eye can inspect it without a prodigious amazement'. And there, on the first page, is 'POEM', in the largest roman capitals then cut, as big as a poster. Poetry has indeed come down from Parnassus to the arena.

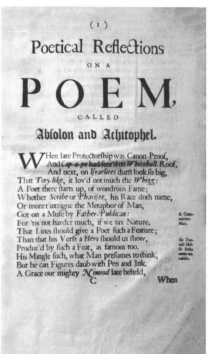

George Villiers, 2nd Duke of Buckingham, *Poetical Reflections on a late Poem*, London, 1681.

Between Neville's *Sentiments* and *Poetical Reflections on a late Poem* appeared another folio book of poetry so far removed from them as to seem come from another world, as indeed it had. *Miscellaneous Poems by Andrew Marvell, Esq; Late Member of the Honourable House of Commons* was printed three years after the poet's death in 1678. It bore a certificate that it was 'Printed according to the exact copies of my late dear Husband, under his own Hand-Writing, being found since his Death among his other papers', subscribed 'Mary Marvell'. Mary Palmer had been his London housekeeper, who successfully claimed to be his widow in a court case over his property, of which she had been left with 'but a few Bookes & papers of a small value'.[14] The publication appears to have been her attempt to profit from them; whether she was indeed married to him is doubtful.[15] No autograph of Marvell's poems exists, so we have only her assertion that the 1681 folio poems are 'exact copies'. The only other witness is another copy, now in the Bodleian,[16] with manuscript corrections, which probably stems from William Popple, Marvell's nephew. These versions may derive from earlier copies in Marvell's hand. What is remarkable (and gives colour to the printed certificate) is the infrequency of the interfering punctuation, even at the end of lines, that we have come to associate with compositorial habit. Capitalisation too is not conventional, but has its own consistency; it is not uniformly applied to substantives, but only those that carry some emphatic force (carrying over to epithets attached to them). Italic type, however rendered in the manuscript, has a special significance: if used conventionally for proper names, it is not otherwise used for extra emphasis, but rather to point antithesis, between two words, two ideas, or even a different language

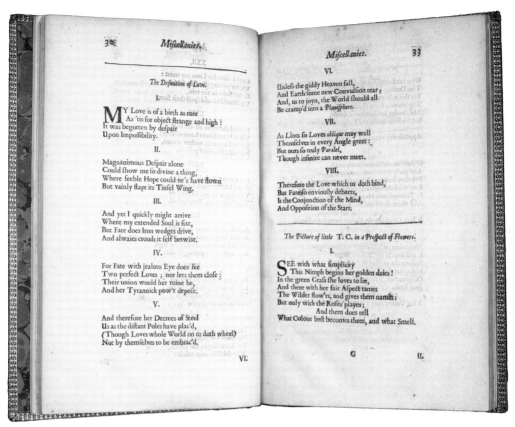

Andrew Marvell,
Miscellaneous Poems,
London, 1681.

from that elsewhere in the poem. 'The Definition of Love' is itself an antithesis: infinite, love cannot be defined, 'begotten by despair / Upon Impossibility'. '*Planisphere*', '*oblique*' and '*Paralel*' are in italic because they are astronomical terms, but the analogy pervades the whole poem. The 'Two perfect Loves' are at opposite poles, separate '(Though Loves whole World on us doth wheel)', only capable of joining if 'the World should all / Be crampe'd into a *Planisphere*', a two-dimensional projection in which the poles are joined by two perfect semicircles, the parentheses that enclose the 'whole World' in (by no coincidence) the longest line in the poem.[17] Marvell, who wrote prose as vivid and precise as his verse (his letters are in a notably bold clear hand), was clearly attuned to the tension between words spoken and read; his use of these *lunulae* is always subtle, as asides, addressed to himself or a reader, a whisper behind the hand while the public discourse goes on.

Poised between ancient and modern, like Janus facing both ways, Marvell had written in an age of scribal circulation, when poets were, with few exceptions, still some removes from the compositor who put their work into print, but with a precision that looked forward to an age when a poet looked directly towards print as the vehicle for his verse. In 1681, the two worlds of script and print coalesced. The *Proclamation for the Better Discovery of Seditious*

Libellers (1676) was directed against those who 'do daily devise and publish, as by Writing, as Printing, sundry false, infamous, and scandalous Libells'.[18] The more dangerous might remain in script rather longer, at least as long as censorship remained, but most of the contents of the successive editions of *Poems on Affairs of State* passed rapidly into print. But the fashion for these topical miscellanies sprang from their previous and contemporary circulation in manuscript, in single sheets or small pocketable books. In print, they became octavos, not folios, preserving a mass of poetry, serious and ribald, from the old panegyrics on Cromwell to the latest ribaldry about the birth of the future Old Pretender.

Rochester was a central figure in this process. Writings originally intended for a small court circle found an increasingly wide readership, finally achieving print in 1680. But what appeared in print was very different from what was available in manuscript. Several, perhaps many, stages of transmission (some perhaps oral rather than scribal) intervened. 'To a Lady: in a Letter', as printed in 1680, is an early six-stanza version. A later version in eight stanzas had already come out, bowdlerised, in *A New Collection of the Choicest Songs* (1676). The manuscript here represents the change between the two, but Rochester clearly composed in his head; four stanzas went down on the first side of the sheet, then two more, but the final flourish is turned into a *signe de renvoi* that marks the last two stanzas for insertion after verse 2, with a similar flourish.[19] Even in 1696, there are only seven stanzas, in a text very different from Rochester's original, part bowdlerised (hence the missing last stanza) but mostly conventionalised. In essence, Rochester's 1696 *Poems* pursued the same path as the miscellanies it resembles. Dryden's *Miscellany Poems*, published by Jacob Tonson in 1684, can be seen as the first such collection designed for initial publication in print; by the time the sixth volume came out in 1709, it was to contain Pope's first work.

Alexander Pope was the first poet to make a profession out of authorship, given new status by the Copyright Act of 1710, the first attempt to give an author rights over his work. Pope's impact on the form of poetry in print, his own and others', and on the book trade generally, deserves a whole book, and mercifully it has got an outstandingly good one, David Foxon's *Pope and the Early Eighteenth-Century Book Trade* (1991). There, for the first time, the full detail of Pope's absorbed fascination with the appearance of his writings in print was unveiled. The stimulus for Pope's involvement with typography clearly came from Holland, indirectly through the popularity in England of the Elzevir and Wetstein editions of the classics (the latter based on the Paris editions 'ad usum Delphini'), and directly through the similar editions that Tonson commissioned from the Dutch master of the new Cambridge University Press, Cornelius Crownfield. Pope clearly knew these books. He was to deal with three printers – John Watts, William Bowyer and John Wright – and three book-sellers, Jacob Tonson, Bernard Lintot and Lawton Gilliver. The first two printers were outstandingly good, and taught Pope as much as he them. Of the booksellers, Tonson was too good for Pope, so he betook himself to Lintot, whose ambition to supplant Tonson made him more pliable. Gilliver and Wright (the latter succeeding Pope's friend, John Barber, future Lord Mayor) became Pope's tools, following his instructions to the letter.

The first outward sign of Pope's obsession with the appear-ance of his writings comes with the manuscript of *The Pastorals*, written in 1704. Although his writing, unbelievably precise, is clearly modelled on print, the layout is different in one important respect: the roles of italic and roman are reversed. The manu-script has no title-page, but it seems possible that the printed title-page, which appears rather oddly towards the end of *Poetical Miscellanies* (1709), was his invention. There is no mistaking his hand in the heading to the first 'Pastoral'. The fair copy of *An Essay on Criticism*, written in 1709[20] and printed in 1711, is even more revealing. His typographic heading is reproduced on the title-page, including the extra wide letter-spacing of 'ESSAY' and its gouged A, with extraordinary fidelity – so much so as to pose the question which came first. The copy sent to the printer has changed to a neat italic script, with no trace of type. Pope's deter-mination to achieve the effect he wanted was unrelenting; the equivalent pages of his 1717 *Works* show the picture in his mind's eye already in 1704. This is even clearer in the layout of the first 'Pastoral' in 1709 and 1717.

The Rape of the Lock (1714) was Pope's first venture with Lintot. It was a modest octavo, but with six plates by Claude du Bosc after Louis du Guernier, no doubt directed by Pope; it also had an engraved headpiece and initials to each canto, provided by Lintot (they had been used before for Joseph Trapp's inaugural lecture as Professor of Poetry at Oxford in 1711). It was Pope's first major success, selling three thousand copies in four days, the second edition following at once 'tho' not in so fair a manner as the first impression'.[21]

Encouraged by this, Pope embarked on a still greater adven-ture, the translation of Homer. Here he was even more clearly in command. Spence's *Anecdotes* records that 'Ogilby's translation of Homer was one of the first large poems that ever Mr Pope read, and he still spoke of the pleasure it then gave him, with a sort of rapture only on reflecting on it. "It was that great edition with pictures. I was then about eight years old".'[22] It left a strong

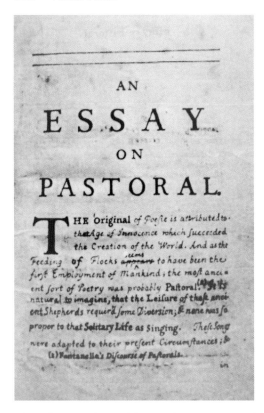
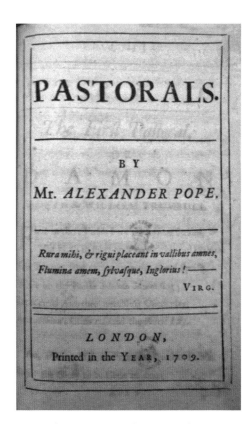

Alexander Pope, 'Pastorals' manuscript, and in *Poetical Miscellanies*, London, 1709.

mark on Pope's plans now. There were to be two editions, one for subscribers in quarto (a revolutionary break with tradition) and another for the trade in traditional folio. Ogilby had financed his edition by subscription, the subscribers paying for plates that bore their names. Pope's subscribers paid for books: the frontispieces, engraved head- and tail-pieces and initials remained under Pope's direction. The debt to Ogilby can be clearly seen in the design of the initials. Although Pope made a fair copy as before, it was not that but an earlier, much rougher draft that served as copy for the printer; he was confident by now that his wishes about the appearance of the page could be met without an exact layout. Besides, he could not have supplied the decorative detail of the subscribers' edition, dictated by the engraved headpieces and initials. The complication of two different page sizes (although the same setting was used for both) was another factor that must have obviated the need for visual directions.

The publication of Pope's Homer, which stretched on to 1726, was a success that dwarfed that of any previous poetic enterprise in the English language. It was followed by other decorated classics – Trapp's *Aeneid* (1718), the 1720 Milton, Pope's Shakespeare (1723–25) and that of Sir Thomas Hanmer (1743) – but it was the quarto format that was an even greater and more pervasive revolution. Folio, as the normal vehicle for poetry, disappeared

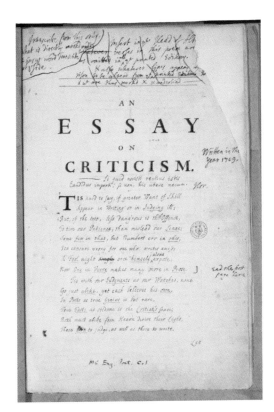

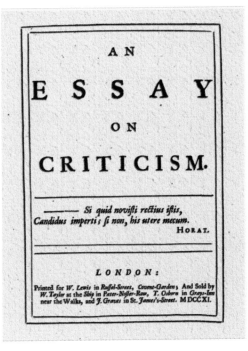

Pope, *An Essay on Criticism*, Oxford, Bodleian Library, Eng. poet. d. 49, and in print, London, 1711.

Iliad I: Ogilby's plate and Pope's initial (D. Foxon, *Pope and the early eighteenth-century book trade*, rev. and ed. J. McLaverty, Oxford, 1991, 40).

within a few years (although Pope's 1717 *Works* retained the
older format, perhaps deliberately), and more and more poetry
appeared in quarto, poetry popularised by Pope's young protegé,
Robert Dodsley. Finally, it is remarkable that Pope, so careful
about appearance, was quite casual where we might expect even
greater precision, over the text. He still expected the compositors
to supply punctuation and italic for proper names, although he
marked italic and capitals for emphasis. This did not stop him
altering all these in proof, and the text as well (his genius was too
fertile to be consistent); over the years he steadily turned against
the marking of emphasis, although it never disappeared. If incon-
sistent in practice, his treatment of these supplements to the text
shows a new awareness of the complement that they created to
the bare words of the text.

In the same year as *Poetical Miscellanies* (1709) Swift published
his first recorded poem, 'Baucis and Philemon'.[23] He had written
it three years earlier, but it was extensively altered at the sugges-
tion of Addison, who found the opening, with the rude reception of the saints, too low. The original is preserved in the fair
copy that Swift made for his friend Sir Andrew Fountaine.[24]
The printed text, issued in ballad form 'Price Twopence', has
the first eight lines alike, but then diverges, skipping forty lines
in the draft. Where the text is the same, the two are so alike,
even in accidentals, as to make it certain that the printer's copy
came direct from Swift; unlike Pope, there is very little italic.
Like Swift, Allan Ramsay made use of a traditional medium, in
his case a traditional Scots song, 'Busk ye, busk ye, my bonny
Bride', and perhaps because the tune was running in his head
wrote his new 'Song' unpunctuated.[25] It is thus conventionally pointed and the capitals of all but proper names removed,
but the spelling ('hastylie', 'Hast ye') is clearly Ramsay's. The
verbal changes ('To westlin breezes' for 'When Zypher Breaths /
Kisses') show him consciously avoiding classical turns for native
phrases.

All the autograph that survives of Samuel Johnson's two great
poems, *London* (1738) and *The Vanity of Human Wishes* (1749),
was preserved in the Hyde collection at Four Oaks Farm.[26] For
London, Johnson evidently folded folio sheets in four to pocketable size, writing down one half long side and then the other.
For *The Vanity of Human Wishes* he cut the sheets in half along the
short side, using them like a booklet, writing first on the rectos
and using the versos for additions. The last lines are written in a
small notebook of the same size, bound in marbled paper covers;
evidently others found this pocket format convenient. Johnson
had a very good memory, and was capable of committing large
parts of what he composed to it before he wrote them down, so

Samuel Johnson, *The Vanity of Human Wishes*, London, 1749, manuscript, Harvard University, Houghton Library.

his drafts are both in effect *aides memoires*. There is nothing to suggest that the manuscripts of either served as printer's copy; he was clearly very economical with paper, but that may have been more a matter of convenience if he kept the sheets on him. Submitting *London* to Edward Cave, publisher of the *Gentleman's Magazine*, he wrote: 'I do not doubt but you will look over this poem with another eye, and reward it in a different manner, from a mercenary bookseller, who counts the lines he is to purchase, and considers nothing but the bulk.'[27] This did not prevent him counting the lines in *The Vanity of Human Wishes*. Although the texts as published vary considerably from the manuscript texts, none of the alterations disturb the total line-count, and the changes could have been introduced in proof. He only hesitates over 'Galileo'; perhaps he first thought of 'Gadbury', the English astrologer, then found it would not scan. His own capitalisation is moderate, and there is no underlining for italic; the compositor probably supplied both, with italic reserved for proper names. Johnson hardly punctuates at all, not surprising if it was all held in his head. There is a colon after 'Lord' (*London* 16.12), where he put a point, and a query after 'view' (*Vanity* 13.7, 143), where he has a comma; neither is an improvement. The manuscript of *Vanity* bears out what Johnson told Boswell about his verses: 'I have generally had them in my mind, perhaps fifty at a time, walking up and down my room; and then I have written them down, and often, from laziness, have written only half lines'.[28] The second halves were clearly added later.

In the decade in which Pope died, Gray composed his *Elegy wrote in a Country Churchyard*, the poem that initiates the Romantic movement, yet disguises its novelty in retrospection. Johnson's strong, instantly recognisable, upright hand could hardly be more different from Gray's neat, very sloping copper-plate. The Eton College manuscript of the *Elegy* is the earliest of three autograph drafts, and alone contains marks of composition, though only one or two changes were written *currente calamo*. Both capitalisation and punctuation are preserved in print, and the changes (comma after 'Darkness', commas omitted after 'Save', s for z in 'drowsy', elision of e in 'Tow'r' and 'Bow'r' and 'sacred' for 'secret') could well have been introduced in proof. What is more striking is the

Thomas Gray, *Elegy wrote in a Country* Churchyard, manuscript, Eton College, and in print, London, 1751.

old-fashioned appearance of the print, unlike the manuscript. The bold heading and still bolder initial, most of all the strip of funerary ornament, straight off a Bill of Mortality, hark back to the beginning of the century. These features must be deliberate, and, since Gray sent the text when finished to Horace Walpole, already engaged with Dodsley, the publisher, on a more sophisticated typographical experiment,[29] it is interesting to speculate whose idea it was to give Gray's nostalgic meditations this antique form.

The difference between the *Elegy* and the quarto editions in his new type that John Baskerville brought out at Birmingham in the same decade could not be more absolute. If Gray's page looks back, Baskerville's is defiantly modern. If the layout and letter-spacing owe much to the Foulis press in Glasgow, the novel types that captivated Europe were all his own design. They needed, and got, better press-work, and the innovation of James Whatman's wove paper, if less obvious, brought about an even more pervasive and long-lasting change. The impact of the Baskerville classics on the presentation of verse could not have been more immediately striking. Edward Capell, in his *Prolusions* (1760), applied it to ancient English literature. Dryden Leach, who was Capell's and also Wilkes's printer, was quick to imitate the new clean typography.

The new style was as quickly absorbed elsewhere in the provinces. The words of John Byrom's hymn, written for Christmas

Catulli, Tibulli et Propertii Opera, Birmingham, John Baskerville, 1772.

1749, have much of the familiarity of the *Elegy*. Byrom was a Manchester man, a poet who invented a short-hand system, and a great book-collector who left his library and manuscripts to Chetham's Hospital in his home town. Not surprisingly, his *Miscellaneous Poems* (1773) was as handsomely printed in octavo by J. Harrop of Manchester as Baskerville's or Leach's quartos in Birmingham and London. The text in the original manuscript was evidently revised before this definitive form. The new appearance disguises its author's conservative capitals, and the conventional pointing of his unpunctuated draft. But again the author's spelling and capitals have been preserved.[30]

The emergence of Robert Burns at the end of the century comes like some great force of nature, overturning so many of the conventions of his time. The image of Burns as yet another 'ploughboy poet' has caused the Kilmarnock first edition of his poems (1786) to be written off as 'provincial'. But 'provincial' is no derogatory term, and Burns's further great success and the many more editions it brought was due to the circulation achieved by the first. 'Ploughboy', too, is a misnomer; Burns's vernacular verse is as artful as Allan Ramsay's. More important still, the time and care he bestowed on rescuing the traditional songs that inspired his own were greater than Ramsay's; and he treated his originals with more respect than Walter Scott did later. He can also be credited with establishing the semi-phonetic rendering of Scots dialect, that Ramsay had begun, in the form familiar today. To these familiar achievements can be added another, not so far noticed, but of special interest to us. He was the first poet to make a regular habit of distributing his autograph; indeed, he can be said to have invented the practice. Hitherto, the survival of rough drafts or fair copies has been due to chance. There are more copies of Burns's poems in his own hand than of any other poet, before or since. People in his own time, as well as since, wanted to feel the sense of immediacy that came from reading verse with such intimate appeal in the poet's own hand, and Burns obliged them.

But there was a simpler reason for this abundance. If no ordinary 'ploughboy', at his outset Burns was remote, geographically and (his friend and patron Mrs Dunlop apart) socially, from the conventional means of bridging the gap from manuscript to print. The manuscript copies were first done for those whose opinion and criticism Burns valued, then for others who had liked what they heard and had no other means of preserving it. After his supporters grew to subscribe enough copies to underwrite *Poems, Chiefly in the Scottish Dialect* (1786), autograph sheets were still in demand. Those who did not, envied those who had them; from

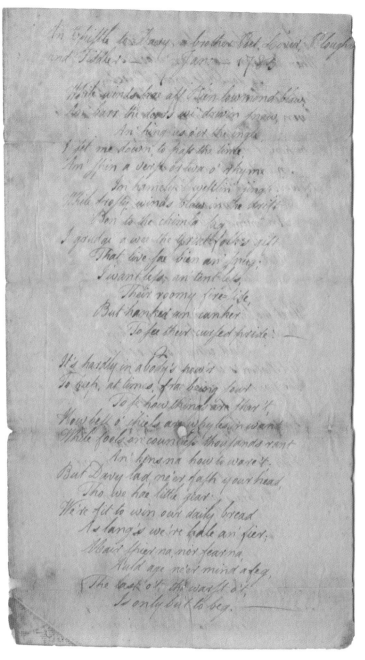

Robert Burns, 'Epistle to Davie, a Brother Poet', manuscript, Rosenbach Museum and Library, Philadelphia, and in print, *Poems, chiefly in the Scottish dialect*, Kilmarnock, 1786.

this it was an easy step to collecting them as mementos and then relics.

The 'Epistle to Davie, a Brother Poet' survives in a manuscript that bears all the signs of having been passed from hand to hand, faded and stained in the process. It was printed in 1786, and there is a new reading, not the English 'fool' (MS) but 'coof', Scots for the same; it may also be significant that 'westlin', a word introduced in Ramsay's song, is italicised. Burns was not the only one

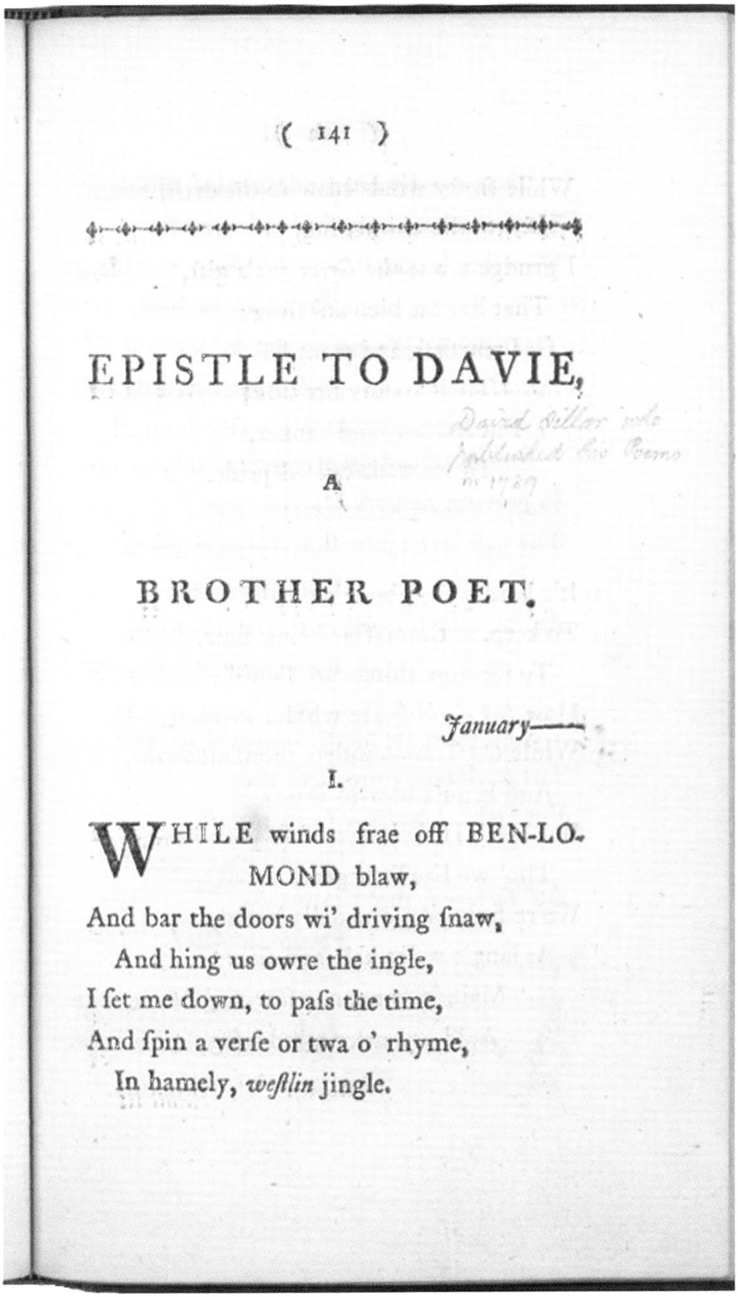

(141)

EPISTLE TO DAVIE,

A

BROTHER POET.

David Sillar who published his Poems in 1789

January——

I.

WHILE winds frae off BEN-LO-
MOND blaw,
And bar the doors wi' driving ſnaw,
And hing us owre the ingle,
I ſet me down, to paſs the time,
And ſpin a verſe or twa o' rhyme,
In hamely, *weſtlin* jingle.

to copy out his verses. His friend and patron Mrs Dunlop copied out 'The Brigs of Ayr' into her copy of *Poems* 1786; it showed Burns's equal mastery of the conventional heroic couplets that so many poets had inherited from Pope. It was first printed in the second, Edinburgh, edition of *Poems* (1787).

Conversely, Burns was now able to explore a wider range of printed outlets: his poems began to appear in newspapers, and as editor of both the *Scots Musical Museum* and *A Select Collection of*

Original Scotish Airs he was able to expand the range of traditional songs that he collected as well as those he wrote, and present both in a form in which they could be sung as well as read. The circle of good fellows singing in chorus at the inn fire became a far wider audience, with the new fortepiano in accompaniment. 'For a' that', as written in Burns's by now practised and beautiful fair copy hand, underwent considerable change as engraved with its proper air, changes adapting it for a wider audience to whom Scots was unfamiliar.[31]

6
The Muse Conscious of Form

The change that Baskerville wrought in typography generally was immediate and striking. The revolution that Pope had begun was complete. Italic, capitals, all were gone; only the punctuation remains unchanged. Decoration had been given a new vitality in Paris, in the form of new printers' flowers, by P.-S. Fournier, who also solved some of the typographic problems implicit in the irregular line-length of verse with his condensed 'oeil poétique' types. But Baskerville had shown the whole of literate Europe that the printed page did not have to be ornate to be handsome. Young's *Night Thoughts*, the most famous of all English poems then, the only one read all over Europe, shows what was to be changed. The comparatively sober English page was given the full rococo treatment for a bilingual text printed in Marseilles. The even more bizarre bilingual edition printed in Germany shows how little popular perception of what the page ought to look like had changed there since the sixteenth century.

It was not the least part of the typographic revolution inaugurated by Baskerville to break this mould. Klopstock's *Messias* (1749) was the first German poem to achieve a reputation outside Germany, if not equal to that of Young's *Night Thoughts*. It has a more elegant page than the Brunswick printer achieved for the bilingual *Night Thoughts*, but still firmly locked in the old tradition. The rigid mould of German typography presented another problem: it had no equivalent of italic, and when emphasis or display required it the want was supplied by letter-spacing the ordinary fraktur lower-case, an inelegant substitute. Goethe, who himself wrote a very modern sloped German script, appears to have been untroubled by it, or the underlying conflict between a still gothic typography and the 'roman' used everywhere outside the Germanic world, and, indeed, for books in Latin printed in Germany. The subject matter, rather than any aesthetic preference, seems to have directed the choice of typography for his works. Only in Frederick the Great's Berlin was there any sign of change, and his favourite Christian von Kleist's *Der Frühling* was given the same treatment as the royal press gave to Voltaire.

The meeting of Goethe and Schiller marked an epoch in this, as in German literature as a whole. It was Schiller who effectually changed the typography of German poetry, even if it took another

LE
LAMENTAZIONI,
O SIA
LE NOTTI
DI YOUNG.

PRIMA NOTTE,

Indirizzata a M. ARTHUR ONSLOW,
Oratore della Camera delle Comuni.

LE MISERIE DELL'UMANITA'.

 OLCE sonno, tu il cui balsamo
ristora l'indebolita natura! .. ohimé
m'abbandona. Simile *anch' egli* al
mondo corrotto, schiva gli sventu-
rati: puntuale a portarsi in que'
luoghi, ove la fortuna è ridente, sen fugge con

LES
COMPLAINTES
OU
LES NUITS
D'YOUNG.

PREMIERE NUIT,

Adressée à M. ARTHUR ONSLOW,
Orateur de la Chambre des Communes.

LES MISERES DE L'HUMANITÉ.

 OUX sommeil, toi dont le
baume répare la nature épui-
sée.... Hélas! il m'abandonne.
Semblable au monde corrompu,
il fuit les malheureux. Exact à se rendre
aux lieux où sourit la fortune, il évite d'une

A ij

---

6   ❋ ❋ ❋

THE
COMPLAINT.

NIGHT THE FIRST.

ON
LIFE, DEATH,
AND
IMMORTALITY.

TO THE RIGHT HONOURABLE
ARTHUR ONSLOW, *Esq;*
SPEAKER OF THE HOUSE OF COMMONS.

T IR'D Nature's sweet Restorer, balmy *Sleep!*
He, like the World, his ready Visit pays
Where Fortune smiles; the Wretched he
forsakes:
Swift on his downy Pinions flies from Woe,
And lights on Lids unsully'd with a Tear.   5

From

* Diesem ehrwürdigen Freunde der Musen und des Vaterlandes hat auch Thomson seinen Herbst zugeeignet. Wie sehr er den erstern Namen verdiene, kann man schon aus dem schliessen, was Thomson von seiner Verdienstkeit sagt, die süsser, als der Gesang seiner Muse, sey; und was Dr. Newton in der Vorrede zu seinem Milton rühmt, daß er ihm zur Ausgabe desselben mit einigen nützlichen Anmerkungen behülflich gewesen. Und wie sehr ihm der andre zukomme, beweist der allgemeine Beyfall der Nation, womit er seit vielen Jahren sein wichtiges Amt verwaltet hat.

[Vers

7

Klagen.
Erste Nacht.

Von
Leben, Tod,
und
Unsterblichkeit.

Dem
Hrn. Arthur Onslow, Esq;
Sprecher im Unterhause, zugeeignet.*

D Er müden Natur süßes Labsal, balsamischer
Schlaf! Ach! er besucht, gleich der Welt, nur
diejenigen gern, denen das Glück zulächelt;
die Elenden verläßt er; fliegt auf seinen weichen Fittigen
schnell vom Jammer hinweg, und — senkt sich auf Au-
genlieder herab, die keine Thräne befleckt.

𝕬 4   Ich

[Vers 1. u. f.] Gleichwie sich dieses ganze Werk von allen Lehr-
gedichten überhaupt, und ins besondre von denen, worinn eben
die Materien abgehandelt sind, vorzüglich unterscheidet: So
weicht auch schon der Anfang desselben von der gewöhnlichen Art
der Einleitungen sehr ab. Er ist dramatisch; und er muß noth-
wendig jeden Leser zum wenigsten eben so aufmerksam machen,
und mit keiner geringern Erwartung erfüllen, als der pathetische
Anfang eines schönen Trauerspiels, z. E. einer Euripidischen
Iphigenia in Aulis, oder einer Crebillonischen Electra,
thun könnte; und diese Erwartung, so groß sie auch seyn mag,
wird

century to complete the revolution. He wrote a singularly beautiful hand himself. His *Musen-Almanach* (1798) was published by Cotta, the first publisher to achieve a truly national market for his wares, in roman type, even if *Wallenstein* (1800), a vernacular subject, reverts. *Die Jungfrau von Orleans* (1802) was printed by Christian Friedrich Unger, with a roman title-page but the text in a curious bastard roman-fraktur type. The breakthrough of newly legible German was immediate. Bürger's *Leonora* was an instant success in England; Scott's first publication was a translation from the already popular Bürger, William Sotheby translated *Oberon*, and Coleridge *Wallenstein*.

Edward Young, *Night Thoughts*, in parallel German and English, and French and Italian.

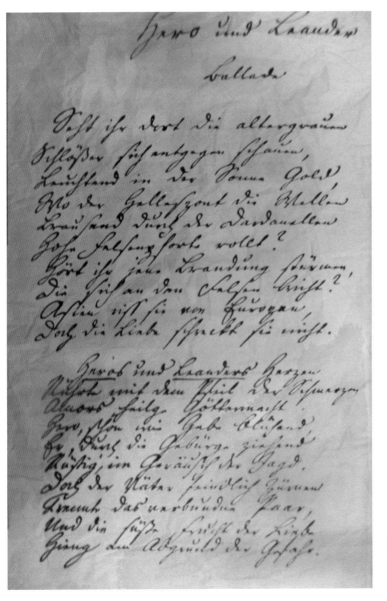

Friedrich Schiller, manuscript and (*overleaf*) in print, *Musen-Almanach für das Jahr 1797*.

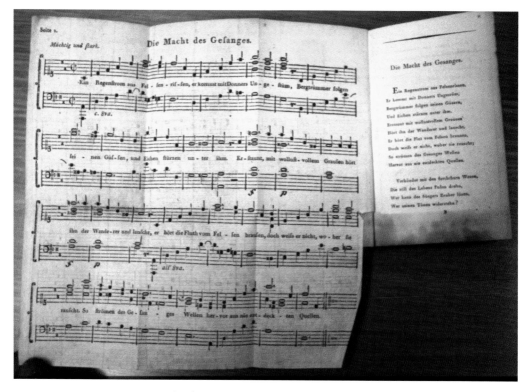

If change came late to Germany, the revolution that Baskerville inspired swept Europe. His own types were bought by Beaumarchais and used by him at Kehl, conveniently beyond the reach of French censorship, for his own most famous work, *La Folle Journée* (adapted by Lorenzo da Ponte as the libretto for Mozart's *Le Nozze di Figaro*) and for the great complete edition of the works of Voltaire; finally they were used for *Le Moniteur*, the organ of Revolution itself. But long before that, other hands had pursued the change in the form of letters to its logical conclusion. The substitution of the 'modern face' for the 'old face' type, derived from the Italian humanist hand and going back like it to the fifteenth century, was the acknowledged achievement of the brothers Pierre-François and François-Ambroise Didot. They, even more than Giovan Battista Bodoni (marooned in ducal splendour at Parma, so more admired than employed by the book trade at large), allied classical purity of design to even finer press-work and paper. The Didot types were quickly imitated by all the type-founders in Europe, even in Italy, where Bodoni's spectacular but inaccessible example produced instant imitation.

Giuseppe Parini (1729–99), poised between the *ancien régime* and revolution, preferred that his works should circulate in manuscript, taking advantage of this to alter and adapt them. But finally, the demand for fair copies was too much. The *Odi* were printed at Milan in a definitive edition in 1791, followed the same year by

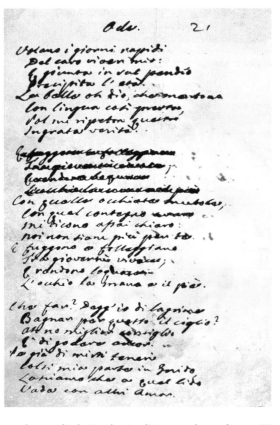

Con quelle occhiate mutole
Con quel contegno avaro
Mi dicono assai chiaro:
Noi non siam più per te.

E fuggono e folleggiano
Tra (1) gioventù vivace;
E rendonvi (2) loquace
L'occhio la mano e il piè.

Che far? Degg'io di lagrime
Bagnar per questo il ciglio?
Ah no; miglior consiglio
È di godere ancor.

Se già di mirti teneri
Colsi mia parte in Gnido,
Lasciamo che a quel lido
Vada con (3) altri Amor.

LEZIONI VARIE.

(1)   Con
(2)   E rendono loquace
       L'occhio la mano il piè.
(3)   Vada co gli altri Amor.

Giuseppe Parini, *Il Brindisi*, manuscript and in print, *Opere*, Milan, 1801–4.

an elegant little Bodoni edition and another at Piacenza. But there were several manuscript texts of 'Il Brindisi', and in the definitive posthumous edition of his works (1801) these multiple versions now required *variae lectiones*, like a classical author.

Britain was rather slower to follow the rest of Europe into neo-classicism, not now because it lagged behind in technical skill but because the example of Baskerville was strong. The Kilmarnock Burns is a handsome piece of printing set in the Bristol-based type-founder Fry's imitation of Baskerville's type, with an awareness of the new French decorative taste. The evolution towards the 'modern face' in Britain was thus slower, but the transition produced some of the most beautiful poetic pages ever printed. *Poems by Goldsmith and Parnell*, printed by William Bulmer in 1795, stands at this point. It is a piece of conscious artistry, English poetry given classic status. No trace of the original apparatus of capitalised nouns and italic proper names remains; even the punctuation is modernised. If logic would dispute some of the terminal commas, this was a tradition that was to last longer.[1] The generously spaced lines, enhanced by Bewick's woodcuts, convey that poetry is no longer another genre of literary expression, another article of trade, but something more elevated. It was to find a new market, and even a new format, in a now

Sir Walter Scott, *The Lady of the* Lake, manuscript, New York, Pierpont Morgan Library MA 443 (Croft 96), and in print, Edinburgh, 1810.

industrial age. Robert Bloomfield, a genuine ploughboy poet, owed much to the example of Bulmer's *Goldsmith and Parnell*. Rejected by every publisher, he made his fair copy in imitation of the printed form he had hoped it might achieve. Chance (and his patron Capel Lofft) provided it, and the poet saw his carefully marked small capitals and italic realised in print, complete with Bewick woodcuts.

The Lay of the Last Minstrel had made Walter Scott famous, but *The Lady of the Lake* (1810) created a European sensation. Already, the new typography was dominant in Edinburgh, even down to the heading in the old black-letter, now a mere subsidiary differential. Scott wrote fast, ideas coming to him as he wrote (in line 2, 'sla' – 'slants', perhaps? – became 'shades' as he wrote), and revised what he wrote. He did not initially bother with punctuation, even omitting the apostrophe in 'bowd' and 'touchd'; only the last query was written *currente calamo*. The bold commas and semi-colons, and especially the long dash after line 5 indicating

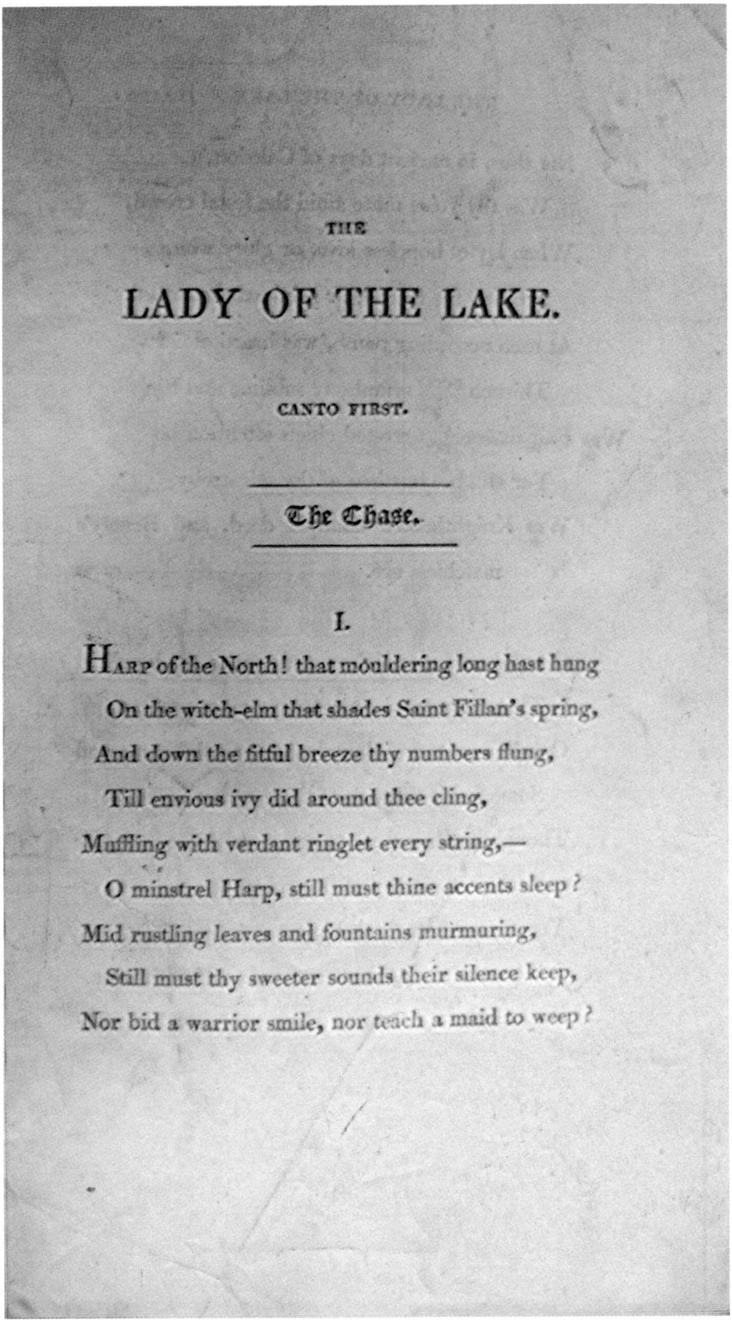

THE

LADY OF THE LAKE.

CANTO FIRST.

𝕿𝖍𝖊 𝕮𝖍𝖆𝖘𝖊.

I.

Harp of the North! that mouldering long hast hung
  On the witch-elm that shades Saint Fillan's spring,
And down the fitful breeze thy numbers flung,
  Till envious ivy did around thee cling,
Muffling with verdant ringlet every string,—
  O minstrel Harp, still must thine accents sleep?
Mid rustling leaves and fountains murmuring,
  Still must thy sweeter sounds their silence keep,
Nor bid a warrior smile, nor teach a maid to weep?

the break in syntax after the comma, have been inserted by Scott's printer, James Ballantyne. But, as the printed page shows, Scott, if he wrote too fast to punctuate as he wrote, was not indifferent: the query in line 6 and comma in the following line must be authorial alterations, heightening the more direct apostrophe to the harp beginning after the dash. Other substantive corrections in stanzas 2 and 3 attest his thorough proof-reading. So it is not only the typography that is new. The old 'conventional' typography has been exchanged for an intelligent dialogue between printer and poet.

Coleridge had a similar relationship with Joseph Cottle at Bristol, another equally talented provincial printer. The copy that he set from was the 'Rugby MS.', now at Texas. The poems in it had been revised before Cottle managed to extract it from Coleridge in August 1795, and he continued to revise them up to a week or two before *Poems on Various Subjects* was published on 16 April 1796, and after the manuscript returned to him. The poem as then printed was headed 'Composed August 20th, 1795, at Clevedon, Somersetshire', finally becoming 'The Eolian Harp' in 1817. Addressed to Sara Fricker, whom he was to marry in October 1795, it was Coleridge's favourite poem then, the vehicle for kaleidoscopic emotions. It is clear that Cottle took Coleridge's original draft seriously (preserving the eccentric spelling 'diversly'). But all Coleridge's now rather old-fashioned capitals have gone, except for the magic 'Lute' itself, soon to become the 'organic Harp' (to be seen emerging in the last but

Samuel Coleridge, 'Composed at Clevedon', manuscript, MS Rugby, University of Texas at Austin (Croft 97), and in print in *Poems*, London, 1797.

one line of the cancelled passage). Unlike Scott, he marked the apostrophe in 'fram'd' and 'thro''. Where the responsibility for the punctuation lies is not so clear; the added semi-colon and commas may be conventional, but the exclamation mark after 'Lute' and the query carefully transferred to 'God of all' (this line is all that was salvaged from the cancelled passage), suggest otherwise. Cottle and Coleridge were rather closer than Scott and Ballantyne (Coleridge wrote a poem for Cottle to address to him), so the responsibility may indeed be joint.

The actual sheet on which Byron, still enthralled by first sight of his beautiful cousin, Mrs Wilmot, dashed down the letter, one of the most famous love-letters in the English language, survives. What others lie between, what form did emotion recollected, not perhaps in tranquillity but just later, take, before it was frozen on the severely neo-classical pages of *Hebrew Melodies* (1815)? There are enough changes – 'gaudy', changed to 'garish', reverts – to show that Byron revised what he originally wrote, in copy or proof. Dashes, when thought outran the pen, were a common substitute for punctuation in letters, and Byron has six; nothing else crossed his mind. Conventional punctuation was, rather laboriously, substituted in print. The comma after 'Beauty' is good, heightening the enjambment that follows, but the capitals of

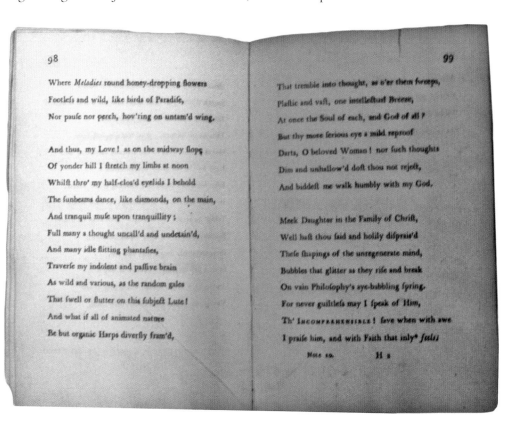

'Beauty', 'Night', 'Goodness', 'Sweetness' and, small but unmistakable, 'Love', are a sad loss. One clear printer's error took place,
and has lasted to this day. The second stanza begins 'One shade
the more, one ray the less'. The third, in Byron's script (now
or later), echoes it: 'And on that cheek, and on that brow'. The
compositor misread 'on' as 'oer' (no apostrophe, like Scott), and
'o'er' it has remained. It's absurd: a shadow may pass over a brow,
but a tint glows *on* it. The compositor might have known better if
the last stanza, infinitely revealing but unfinished, had been before
him, with the tell-tale old-fashioned apostrophe in 'It's'.

Keats was far from famous when the 'Ode to Autumn' came
to him on 19 September 1819 at Winchester on his Sunday walk;
he was en route to Rome and death when it was published in
Lamia and Other Poems in 1820. The sole surviving draft suggests
that he had the first stanza complete in his head when he got
back to his lodgings, and only then began to draft the second and
third; the second was more or less finished, the third less so.[2] This
sheet was sent to his brother George; writing to his friends John
Hamilton Reynolds and Richard Woodhouse on 21 September,
he transcribed the poem.[3] Another fair copy must have gone to
the printer. Although writing at speed, fearful lest the magic lines
escape, so fast that he makes lots of spelling mistakes, his punctuation is exact. An interesting example comes in line 4 of the first
stanza, where he puts in a colon (semi-colon in print) not after
the last word where it belongs, but after the preceding word, clear
evidence that his mind was running ahead of his pen. The substantive changes ('sweet' for 'white') show that the final copy was
revised; it is possible, then, that the punctuation is all Keats's, even
the comma at the end of line 8, which is picked up by the comma
after the second 'more', in the next line. The most striking feature
of the draft, however, is the careful indentation, which reflects
the rhyming lines. The rhyme scheme is subtle: *ababcdecdde*, with
each new end-rhyme signalled by an extra indent. But in the first
stanza the rhyme scheme is different: *ababcdedcce*. This disturbs the
indentation in the draft; the eighth line, which rhymes with the
sixth, aligns with the fourth, the ninth and tenth correctly with
the fifth, and the seventh and eleventh likewise. How this was
handled in the printer's copy is beyond recovery, but it was too
complicated for the compositor; clearly he did his best to follow
copy, but missed the point of aligning the rhyme-lines. No one
has done better since: the 'Ode' is commonly printed without
indents.

The 'Ode to Autumn' is a remarkable poem in every way.
No one since Pope had set such store by exactitude in matters
of punctuation. The visual linking of rhymes was an innovation,
even if blown off course by Keats's own inspiration, the same

John Keats, 'Autumn', manuscript, Harvard University, Houghton Library (Croft 108–9) and in print in *Lamia and other Poems*, London, 1820.

138   POEMS.

2.

Who hath not seen thee oft amid thy store?
  Sometimes whoever seeks abroad may find
Thee sitting careless on a granary floor,
  Thy hair soft-lifted by the winnowing wind;
Or on a half-reap'd furrow sound asleep,
  Drows'd with the fume of poppies, while thy hook
  Spares the next swath and all its twined flowers:
And sometimes like a gleaner thou dost keep
  Steady thy laden head across a brook;
  Or by a cyder-press, with patient look,
  Thou watchest the last oozings hours by hours.

3.

Where are the songs of Spring? Ay, where are they?
  Think not of them, thou hast thy music too,—
While barred clouds bloom the soft-dying day,
  And touch the stubble-plains with rosy hue;

POEMS.   139

Then in a wailful choir the small gnats mourn
  Among the river sallows, borne aloft
  Or sinking as the light wind lives or dies;
And full-grown lambs loud bleat from hilly bourn;
  Hedge-crickets sing; and now with treble soft
  The red-breast whistles from a garden-croft;
  And gathering swallows twitter in the skies.

wind that disturbed his spelling. The sense of absolute immediacy, the nearness of the ideas forming in the poet's mind to the paper on which they were set down, is as captivating now as it was when Richard Monckton Milnes first felt and expressed it.[4] This is a rather different emotion from that which made people want to possess Burns's poems in autograph. Keats, like Burns, sent drafts to friends whose opinion he valued; sending this sheet to George Keats in America was part of the series of newsletters with which his brother kept him up to date with family news. When George gave the sheet to Miss Anna Barker of New Orleans in 1839, the passion for autograph collection was under way,[5] and Keats on his way to immortality. There is, perhaps, a more technical reason why scraps of paper touched by genius came to be valued now, apart from the sentimental and romantic desire for physical association. There could hardly be three more different poets than Scott, Byron, and Keats, but all three were constrained within the same remarkably similar neo-classical typographic frame – elegant, chaste but cold. Old-style typography may have struck the industrial age as rough, homely, even ungainly, but the old apparatus of capitals, italic and punctuation made the poetry seem more accessible, closer.

Whether it was reaction to a new typography fit for the new industrial age or desire for a new sense of intimate contact with poet as well as poetry, with the nineteenth century came the decorative 'album', in which texts or pictures might be gathered together. In these pride of place went to pieces of verse, if possible in the poet's own hand. As Burns had come to realise, poetry on pieces of paper, ready for the autograph album, came to be a valued supplement to the printed page. It is significant that Lamartine should have inscribed the poems that were to become *Méditations Poétiques* (1820) in such an album, a book already bound, perhaps intended as a pocket sketch-book.[6] The recipient was his muse, Julie Charles, first met in 1816; its neatness here gives it a finished air, but the poem was to be changed considerably before it reached print. Julie's name has disappeared, among a number of substantive alterations. In the manuscript, Lamartine's dropped commas are a little difficult to follow, but the fact that they are used against the sense to mark the alexandrine caesura makes it clear that this is poetry for recitation, not print. This is made even clearer by the emphatic semi-colons in line 4, where there are commas in print. The first sentence ends with a colon there, not the exclamation mark that directed it as an invocation to Julie. The contrast between the urgency of the sloping script, neat though it is, and the monumental rectangularity of the print, heightened by use of an 'oeil poétique' type, could not be more absolute. Lamartine, if a more than fashionable poet, owed much

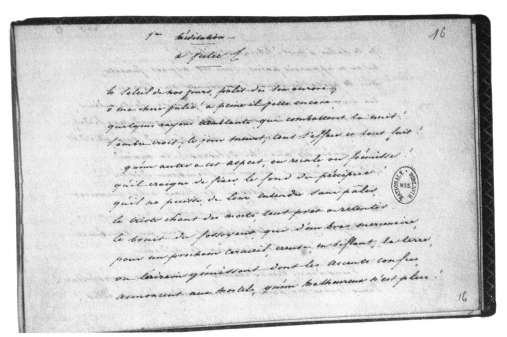

to the complex currents of post-Revolutionary France to which he responded. No one could have been more fashionable than Caroline Norton, the beautiful and hapless daughter of Sheridan, the now forgotten author of 'The Arab's Farewell to his Steed' and 'Not Lost but Gone Before'. Her script was as beautiful as Lamartine's and more decorative. It was thus ideally suited to the pages of albums, for which her books, as popular in America as in England, provided much to copy.

Alphonse de Lamartine, manuscript, Paris, Bibliothèque Nationale, nouv.acq.fr.14013, f.16.

Elizabeth Barrett Browning's 'Sonnets from the Portuguese' had a properly romantic inspiration, although their publication in her *Poems* in two volumes in 1850 could not have been more ordinary. If unromantic, the latter illustrates a new feature of printed verse, the new small format. Scott, Byron and Moore all came out in quarto and quickly transferred to the now more normal but still large octavo. Humbler poets, Bloomfield (even if his first editions were quarto) and Keats, went into small octavo. The posthumous success of Keats was one of the factors that now made small octavo the standard format for books of verse. *Poems* (1850) was no exception. The poet's script, however, was exceptional: her 'swift and fluent cursive possesses a curious grace which is highly individual and at the same time thoroughly feminine',[7] although it could hardly be more different from Mrs Norton's. In Sonnet XIV, the layout and punctuation, too, are idiosyncratic: the vertical alignment of initial capitals is strictly observed, despite the eccentric double quotes (a comma and vertical dash). The double point, neither ellipsis nor dash, is her own invention. When she slips out of quoted speech into direct address to her

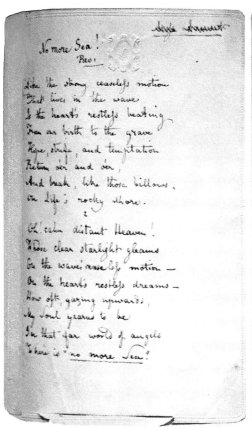
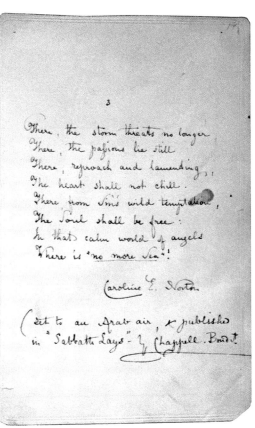

Caroline Norton, 'No More Sea', from her niece Marcia Sheridan's album.

'Beloved', she seems to have imagined herself speaking, but there is no opening quote, and she hesitated over the speech's end, halfway through or at the end of the tenth line.[8] All this confused the compositor, who fudged the double point and semi-colon in line 4 and gave up on the double point in line 8, adding an erroneous terminal comma.

Longfellow's *Hiawatha* (1855), the title providentially changed from 'Manabozho' the year before, was also altered textually a good deal between first draft,[9] written initially on rectos only, and print. The distinctive script, regular even in pencil, is widely spaced, both characteristics that seem to have influenced its translation into typography. The changes all tend towards simplicity. The deleted passage was not lost, for the draft continues with the same lines written out fair and expanded on the next verso. In subject and metre, as in script and print, Longfellow was at pains to break with any existing model, to recapture the ancient 'legends and traditions' of a society pure of the apparatus of an alien tradition of verse and its visible forms.

Fitzgerald, however, faced a more complicated task in a more complicated way. He had already published translations of the classics and Calderon, and had begun to learn Persian from Edward

Cowell when he discovered Omar Khayyám. His first attempt at translation was in 'monkish Latin', an attempt to avoid a tradition of English translation that went back to Collins's *Oriental Eclogues* and the more literal verse of Sir William Jones. Ultimately, he found a diction that suited him, owing little to the original, antique but not archaic. The visible signs, the old-fashioned capitals and 'ye' for 'the', were matched by his hand, whose irregular calligraphy strangely recalls a sixteenth-century hand, such as Sidney's. There is no punctuation in the draft, but the colons and the apostrophe for silent 'e' suggest that Fitzgerald, not the compositor, added it.[10] The resolution of the 'scarcely Persian' 'O Man' shows the conflict from which his style evolved, when it reached the second edition of the *Rubáiyát of Omar Khayyám* in 1868.

If Fitzgerald sought to translate not merely the words but something of the spirit of Persia into his *Rubáiyát*, he could not repeat the fluid grace of its Arabic script. By contrast, the Cyrillic alphabet always looked to its Greek origins, and in its first typographic form repeated its manuscript tradition. In the eighteenth century, however, western European taste prevailed, and the neo-classic typography of the Didot brothers and Bodoni was repeated, with no less grace, in the early works of Aleksandr Pushkin. The manuscript (still preserved in the Institute of Russsian Literature) of 'K' Moryn' ('To the Sea') shows a hand already feeling its way towards print, although the first publication of the poem in the journal *Mnemozyna* 4 (1825) omits the careful stanzaic pattern, lightly but clearly indicated in the poet's fair copy. This was faithfully restored in the definitive edition of the works, *Stikhotvoreniia Aleksandra Pushkina* (1846). Pushkin, who wrote easily and without much revision, found relief or diversion in the engaging pictures that he drew in the margins of what he wrote.

These exotic new ventures must not obscure the fact that two famous Italian poets of the nineteenth century drew inspiration from the oldest of all sources of European poetry, the poetry and myths of ancient Greece and Rome. If Ugo Foscolo (1778–1827) derived the inspiration for *Lettere di Ortis* (1798) from Goethe, his passion for Latin and Greek was independent of such influence. When he left Venice for Milan in 1813, his hand, an aesthetic upright script, found congenial typographic form in the style canonised by Bodoni, which he took with him to England. Leopardi (1798–1837), like Keats and Pushkin, did not live to see the fame that came to him with the publication at Florence of his *Opere* in six volumes in 1845–49. The hand (not unlike that of Foscolo) in which he wrote the poetical address to Cardinal Mai, the great palaeographer who did so much to

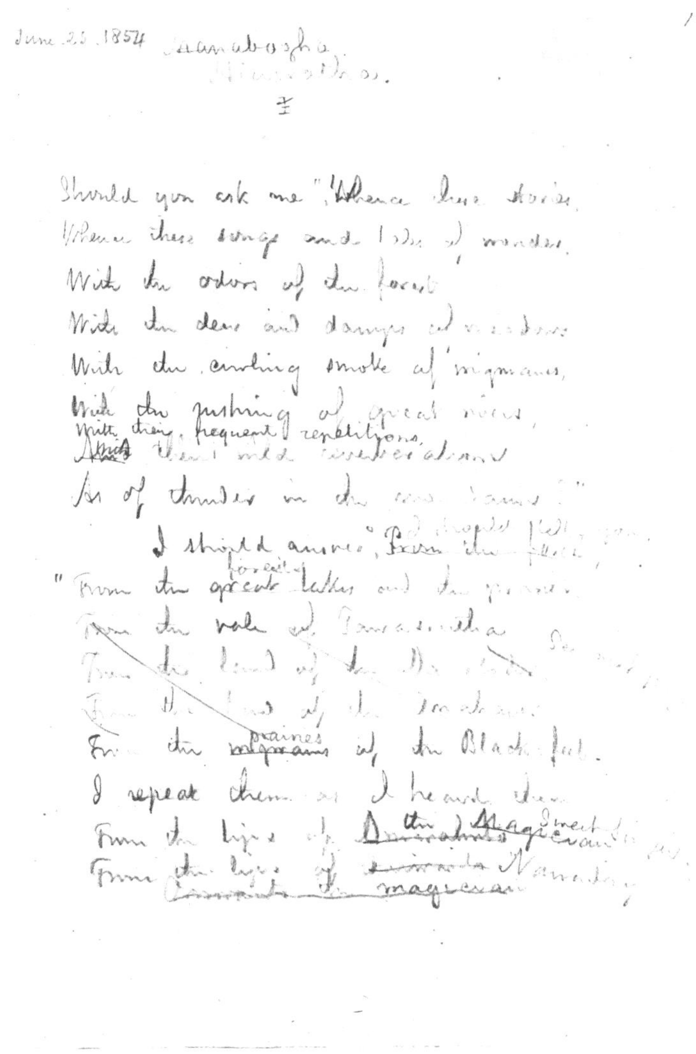

Henry Longfellow,
The Song of Hiawatha,
manuscript, Harvard
University, Houghton
Library (Croft 114), and in
print, London, 1855.

revive the Greek classics and in doing so inspired both Foscolo
and Leopardi, differed little from the same humanistic hand in
which he wrote that most famous of all his poems, the 'Canto
Notturno di un Pastore Errante nell' Asia'. His own punctuation
was careful, as the corrected proof of the poem to Mai reveals; it
was carefully preserved in Antonio Ranieri's posthumous text.[11]
Giosue Carducci (1835–1907) was as steeped in the work of the
earlier Italian poets. His own hand was a consciously calligraphic
form of Italian copper-plate,[12] unaltered even when he exchanged
the severe 'modern face' typography of G. Barbera at Florence,
under whose imprint his early works were published, for the
striking *arte nuova* 'old style' of Nicola Zanichelli at Bologna in
1877. *Odi barbari* set a new style for 'poetic' typography that was
not lost in France.

| 4   THE SONG OF HIAWATHA. | INTRODUCTION.   5 |

From the land of the Ojibways,
From the land of the Dacotahs,
From the mountains, moors, and fenlands,
Where the heron, the Shuh-shuh-gah,
Feeds among the reeds and rushes.
I repeat them as I heard them
From the lips of Nawadaha,
The musician, the sweet singer."
    Should you ask where Nawadaha
Found these songs, so wild and wayward,
Found these legends and traditions,
I should answer, I should tell you,
" In the bird's-nests of the forest,
In the lodges of the beaver,
In the hoof-prints of the bison,
In the eyry of the eagle !
    " All the wild-fowl sang them to him,
In the moorlands and the fenlands,
In the melancholy marshes ;
Chetowaik, the plover, sang them,

Mahng, the loon, the wild goose, Wawa,
The blue heron, the Shuh-shuh-gah,
And the grouse, the Mushkodasa !"
    If still further you should ask me,
Saying, " Who was Nawadaha ?
Tell us of this Nawadaha,"
I should answer your inquiries
Straightway in such words as follow.
    " In the Vale of Tawasentha,
In the green and silent valley,
By the pleasant water-courses,
Dwelt the singer Nawadaha.
Round about the Indian village
Spread the meadows and the corn-fields,
And beyond them stood the forest,
Stood the groves of singing pine-trees,
Green in Summer, white in Winter,
Ever sighing, ever singing.
    " And the pleasant water-courses,
You could trace them through the valley,

Tennyson's 'Oenone' had a long gestation, charted with great insight and clarity by Philip Gaskell.[13] Its impetus came from his journey to the Pyrenees with Arthur Hallam and the landscape there, overlaid upon a long and deep love of the eclogues of Virgil and of Theocritus. Two drafts precede its first publication in *Poems* (Cambridge, 1833), a small book like *Lamia*. Tennyson was pilloried for it, like Keats before him. Although the bones of the poem are there and were to remain unaltered, the mixture of hackneyed phrases and outlandish compounds ('manyfountained' without a hyphen) annoyed his critics. It was heavily revised over almost a decade, six successive drafts following before it reappeared in the two-volume *Poems* (1842), published by Edward Moxon. The most complex of these shows the whole of the opening and its banal phrases struck out, and a new image of the rising mountain mist introduced. Its position and script shows that it follows the revisions lower down. The decision to break line 11, perpetuated in print, had already been taken. Tennyson's punctuation in draft is minimal, and repeated enjambment, a striking and novel feature of his poetry, prevented 'conventional' punctuation. What appears in print reflects sense, not sound, lightly and not so as to

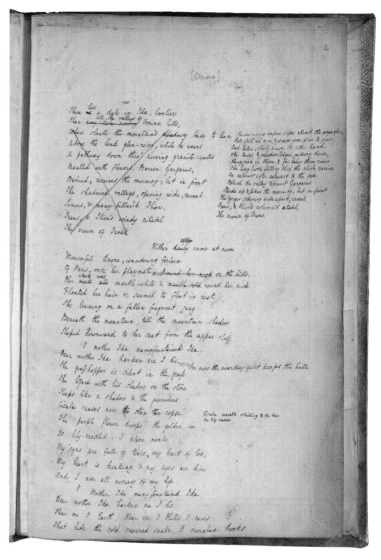

Right and opposite Alfred
Tennyson, 'Oenone',
manuscript, Cambridge,
Trinity College, and in
print in *Poems* 1833 and
1842 (P. Gaskell, *Writer to
Reader*, 128 + 134).

disturb the run from line to line; Tennyson's emphatic colons (at
the foot) are carefully preserved. If not his own, the pointing must
have been added by Moxon, a poet himself.

Up to now, the process by which words in the poet's mind took
visible form, written first on paper, and then transmuted into
print, can be seen as a progress through tension, even contention.
Putting things down on paper may be a step forward, preserving
what would not last beyond human memory, but it is also a
constriction, silencing the aural component. The gain, adding a
visual pattern to words merely spoken or sung, is compounded
by the existence of a record, an irregular line that enables poet or
reader to follow an idea further or retrace it back to its source.

The written line may move from sheet to sheet, broken if a sheet is lost or destroyed, to be restored on another, connection maintained in the link between mind and hand. Print, as Tennyson found, cuts the line into sections, stilling its motion and fixing its form at that point. At the same time it creates, through multiple copies of that form, a lateral movement that increases its audience, whose perception and needs may react with the poet's aims and carry the idea forward in a different direction. Mechanisation of the press and improved communications increased this pressure: the printed page, directed to a less defined body of readers, becomes impersonal, a void that the poet can fill. So, by the mid-nineteenth century, the old conventions disappear, and accidentals become authorial; only the oldest convention, an initial capital for each line, survives. Handwriting is also freed from the tyranny of copper-plate: both Elizabeth Barrett Browning and Longfellow escaped in different ways from this, as from other conventions. Unconstrained by the old link with printed letters, the poet's script became another form of self-expression, as well as the words written.

In the 1860s famous books of poems by Christina Rossetti, Arthur Clough, Swinburne and Browning were published. Both Clough's and Christina Rossetti's were collections of poems written earlier; of these, hers dates from 1848, his from about 1850. Their hands could not be more different, hers a neat Italian copper-plate, his with some of the vigour and antique tendency (he uses the old long 's') of Fitzgerald's. Both were published in 1862,

ŒNONE.

There lies a vale in Ida, lovelier
Than all the valleys of Ionian hills.
The swimming vapour slopes athwart the glen,
Puts forth an arm, and creeps from pine to pine,
And loiters, slowly drawn. On either hand
The lawns and meadow-ledges midway down
Hang rich in flowers, and far below them roars
The long brook falling thro' the clov'n ravine
In cataract after cataract to the sea.
Behind the valley topmost Gargarus
Stands up and takes the morning : but in front
The gorges, opening wide apart, reveal
Troas and Ilion's column'd citadel,
The crown of Troas.

           Hither came at noon
Mournful Œnone, wandering forlorn
Of Paris, once her playmate on the hills.
Her cheek had lost the rose, and round her neck
Floated her hair or seem'd to float in rest,
She, leaning on a fragment twined with vine,
Sang to the stillness, till the mountain-shade
Sloped downward to her seat from the upper cliff.

" O mother Ida, many-fountain'd Ida,
Dear mother Ida, harken ere I die.
For now the noonday quiet holds the hill :
The grasshopper is silent in the grass :
The lizard, with his shadow on the stone,
Rests like a shadow, and the cicala sleeps.
The purple flowers droop : the golden bee
Is lily-cradled : I alone awake.
My eyes are full of tears, my heart of love,
My heart is breaking, and my eyes are dim,
And I am all aweary of my life.

Rossetti's *Goblin Market* with a title-page and binding designed by her brother Dante Gabriel (the 1860s was also the great decade of book-illustration), Clough's *Poems* in the old-face type, newly returned to fashion. Both were published by Macmillan, who had succeeded to Moxon's reputation as the publisher of poetry. In both cases there are changes, both substantive and to accidentals, between manuscript and print: all Clough's changes are clearly authorial; the added comma after 'It may be' in stanza 2 and after 'waves' and 'vain' (the latter instead of a too abrupt semi-colon) add a subtle continuity. The sole change in 'Song', that of Rossetti's colons to semi-colons, may be conventional, and the compositor may well have missed the shy comma after 'haply' in the last line. Different though they are, in each case the poet's control of the text is virtually complete.

Swinburne's *Poems and Ballads* (1866) and Browning's *The Ring and the Book* (1868–69) were both published soon after they were written; unlike the two previous examples, both of these bear signs of being written for printing. The hands could not be more different, Swinburne's irregular scrawl reflecting the conflict between his need to express himself on paper and his dislike (due to a weak wrist) of writing, Browning's decisive and regular script written with great deliberation and special care to make his punctuation clear. 'August' in fact went through considerable revision before it was printed, first in *The Spectator*,[14] and then unaltered four years later in *Poems and Ballads*. The carefully numbered stanzas have been transposed. The redraft of the last two lines of the first stanza (rejecting 'spikes', perhaps not in the poet's hand) and the second line improve it (but I regret 'Between low sunbeams and soft rains' in the second); alteration of the colons to semi-colons may (as with Christina Rossetti) have been the printer's choice.

Browning's introduction to his longest poem, characteristically enjambed with the 'arbitrary distribution of accents' of which his critics complained,[15] is set out with exemplary clarity. Especially interesting are his own reflections on the relation of speaking voices, script and print, the voices echoing in his ear from the seventeenth century, passed down, mute on paper, but now given a new voice by his hand. The contrast is already in the book itself, a mixture of script and type, script at front and back, 'from written title-page / To written index', its contents between 'Put forth and printed, as the practice was, / At Rome, in the Apostolic Chamber's type'. But out of this comes a recognisable voice:

> 'Twas the so-styled Fisc began,
> Pleaded (and since he only spoke in print
> The printed voice of him lives now as then)
> The public Prosecutor – "Murder's proved....[16]

The tensions in Browning's versification result from the stress involved in bridging the gap, conveying the sound of the Fisc's long-dead voice emerging from the Apostolic Chamber's type through his own script to Smith, Elder & Co's compositor, who was to revive it, in different print and paper.

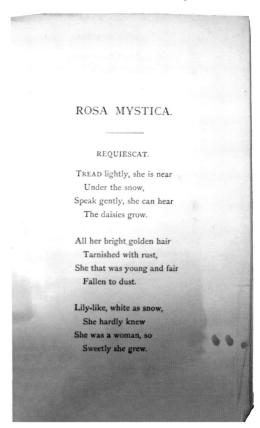

ROSA MYSTICA.

———

REQUIESCAT.

TREAD lightly, she is near
Under the snow,
Speak gently, she can hear
The daisies grow.

All her bright golden hair
Tarnished with rust,
She that was young and fair
Fallen to dust.

Lily-like, white as snow,
She hardly knew
She was a woman, so
Sweetly she grew.

Oscar Wilde, 'Requiescat', manuscript, William Andrews Clark Memorial Library, Los Angeles (Croft 146), and in print in *Poems*, London, 1881.

Oscar Wilde was, perhaps, more sensitive to the aesthetic appearance of words on the page than any previous poet. His own 'Greek and gracious handwriting'[17] makes the little elegy for his long-lost sister beautiful.[18] He took equal care with its printed form in *Poems* (1881), set in the new 'old style' type on a page a little larger than the small 'poetic' octavo, paid for by himself.[19] As with Rossetti, the colons have all gone, now translated into commas. If earlier we may suspect the compositor's hand (nineteenth-century printers' manuals are full of the niceties of punctuation), this time the change must be Wilde's. He was, as usual, in the avant-garde. Fowler, looking back from the next century, wrote, 'As long as the Prayer-Book version of the Psalms continues to be read, the colon is not likely to pass out of use as a stop, chiefly as one preferred by individuals, or in impressive contexts, to the semi-colon'. Such feelings may have suggested the colons in the draft, and likewise the change to commas in the publicity of print.

Stéphane Mallarmé wrote an even more beautiful hand than Wilde.[20] But when *Les Poésies de Stéphane Mallarmé* was finally printed in 1887, in a limited edition issued in nine parts with a frontispiece by Felicien Rops, the poems were lithographed

I

Le vierge, le vivace et le bel aujourd'hui
Va-t-il nous déchirer avec un coup d'aile ivre
Ce lac dur oublié que hante sous le givre
Le transparent glacier des vols qui n'ont pas fui !

Un cygne d'autrefois se souvient que c'est lui
Magnifique mais qui sans espoir se délivre
Pour n'avoir pas chanté la région où vivre
Quand du stérile hiver a resplendi l'ennui.

Tout son col secouera cette blanche agonie
Par l'espace infligée à l'oiseau qui le nie,
Mais non l'horreur du sol où le plumage est pris

Fantôme qu'à ce lieu son pur éclat assigne,
Il s'immobilise au songe froid de mépris
Que vêt parmi l'exil inutile le Cygne .

Stephane Mallarmé, *Les Poésies*, Paris, 1878.

direct from his own fair copies, 'photolithographiées du manuscrit définitif'. He was as exceptional in this as so much else. Even
the ordinary letterpress edition published, with additions, after
his death in 1899 was unusual in being set in italic throughout;
he told his publisher, Edmond Deman, that it was the printed
equivalent of handwriting, which if true to his own hand was
still only a draft, not a definitive text.[21] Mallarmé, again more
sensitive than Wilde to the visible form of words whose rhymes
and complex assonances had to be seen in order to be heard, dealt
with the problem of translating these nuances into print by the
simple method of evading it altogether. It was, however, a challenge not to be ignored: if the cross-linking of sound and meaning
existed in the mind and ear, a visual link with meaning could also
be created, and, since print was the familiar vehicle with which
the eye absorbed meaning, it must be bent to frame the poetic
image. How this was to be done, after centuries in which poetry
had been constrained within a rectangle of script or type within a
larger rectangle of stone, papyrus, vellum or paper, was a problem
he did not live to see solved,[22] but solved it was, in the posthumous edition of *Un coup de dés n'abolira pas le hasard*.

We shall return to this, but *Un coup de dés* was recognised
at once by Paul Claudel as a 'grand poème typographique et
cosmogonique'.[23] He was himself an experimenter, and the publication of *Cinq Grandes Odes* (1910), inspired by Pindar, required a
different kind of typographic innovation. The stanzas of the odes
consisted not so much of lines as ejaculations, too long to be fitted
on a single line, sometimes concluding with a point, at others
running on to the next. His manuscript has an almost liturgical
appearance, each ejaculation beginning a new line with a capital.
It demanded a dignified appearance in type, and (surprising in
France) was given it in Caslon's english roman, the same type
used for Dowson's *Poems*.

In fact, experiment in more modest ways can be seen both
in France and England at the turn of the century. The standard
mould of the nineteenth-century 'poetry book' had broken under
the impact of aestheticism, but no single alternative had taken
its place. Common octavo, undistinguished from other kinds
of books, was the size for Dowson as well as Wilde. The new
calligraphy, equally relieved from the tyranny of 'pothooks and
hangers', went with a tendency to retrospection, as well as regret
for a country life steadily undermined by spreading towns. Thomas
Hardy's *Late Lyrics and Earlier* (1922) reveals all these characteristics. His manuscripts, all fair copies, have their own characteristic and individual grace.[24] It can equally be seen in Carducci's
Odi Barbare, whose manuscripts, also fair copies, have their own
characteristic and individual grace. Typographic dignity is the

THE WILD SWANS AT COOLE
The trees are in their autumn beauty,
The woodland paths are dry,
Under the October twilight the water
Mirrors a still sky;
Upon the brimming water among the stones
Are nine and fifty swans.

The nineteenth Autumn has come upon me
Since I first made my count.
I saw, before I had well finished,
All suddenly mount
And scatter wheeling in great broken rings
Upon their clamorous wings.

I have looked upon those brilliant creatures,
And now my heart is sore.
All's changed since I, hearing at twilight,
The first time on this shore,
The bell-beat of their wings above my head,
Trod with a lighter tread.

Unwearied still, lover by lover,
They paddle in the cold,
Companionable streams or climb the air;
Their hearts have not grown old;
Passion or conquest, wander where they will,
Attend upon them still.

b

William Butler Yeats, 'The Wild Swans at Coole', manuscript, University of Texas at Austin (Croft 152), and in print in *The Wild Swans at Coole*, Churchtown, Cuala Press, 1917.

common feature of their printed pages; the printer, deprived of any role in the text, makes up for it by apt page layout. In more recent time, Giuseppe Ungaretti (1888–1970), who wrote a fine aesthetic hand, lines always drifting to the right and turned up at the end, found them given Bodoniesque dignity; *Il dolore* (1948) was set by Mondadori in Bodoni's own types, a style that owes much to Giovanni Mardersteig's famous edition of D'Annunzio.

Yeats's handwriting, belying its generous and monumental appearance on the page, is notoriously hard to read, his mind too occupied to finish off letters properly. This is a fair copy, but one on which Yeats was still working, although it was already complete in his head. In line 3 of the second stanza the second word was 'swan', a word close to the 'saw' he wanted; 'well' for 'half' anticipates the question 'if you'd only reached 29, how can you be so sure of the other 30?', although Yeats was perhaps preoccupied with the rhythmic problem that changed 'counted' to 'count'. But perhaps the most interesting signs of the poetic mind at work are the prolonged doubt over 'clamorous' (swans are noisy birds, either way), and the absence of half the punctuation.

The intrusion of the typewriter into the process from poetic idea to final form probably long pre-dates the point that we have now reached, but no poet hitherto seems to have regarded it as

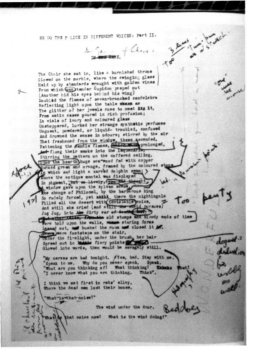

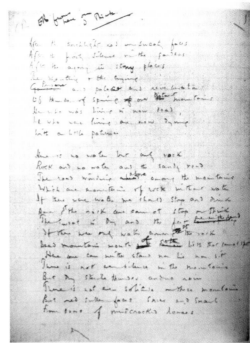

anything other than a useful tool (in other hands) to convey a text already written to the printer, its mechanical clarity obviating the chances of error. As with printers' proofs, it offered a further chance of whetting a word or phrase, and few typescripts are devoid of manuscript correction. But the first poet to have used the typewriter as a means of composition was (I think) Ezra Pound. Bending to his will this intractable source of letters, stringing them together to make not merely the sense he intended but a satisfactory pattern, was the sort of challenge he enjoyed.

But to T.S. Eliot the typewriter was a new tool in 1916. He wrote to Conrad Aiken on 21 August, not about poetry but the reviews and articles he was then writing: 'Composing on the typewriter, I find that I am sloughing off all my long sentences which I used to dote upon. Short, staccato, like modern French prose. The typewriter makes for lucidity, but I am not sure that it encourages subtlety.' He was to discover, in turn, how to make it do that. The evidence of the complex genesis of *The Waste Land*, finally published in 1922, has been set out in Valerie Eliot's fascinating facsimile and transcript of the drafts.[25] The collection of them that eventually came to John Quinn is not in chronological order, even within each section, nor is it easy to see the sequence of alterations, even on any particular sheet. In general, the earliest surviving version is a typescript, on which Vivienne Eliot (as here) commented in pencil. After that, Ezra Pound went over it in detail, clearly on more than one occasion, in pencil and ink. His

T.S. Eliot, *The Waste Land: a Facsimile and Transcript of the Original Drafts including the Annotations of Ezra Pound*, edited by Valerie Eliot, Oxford, 1971, 10 + 70.

remarks, verging from identifying (here wrongly) what he took to be quotations to criticism ('photography?' is an elliptical reference to what he thought was a literal transcription of an overheard conversation), are only intelligible as part of a dialogue that had been going on ever since they met in September 1914. 'Death by Water' once ran to ninety-two lines in Pound's purple typescript, of which only ten found their way into print. What Pound had been transcribing was no doubt the same as Eliot's surviving draft, in pencil on squared paper, of 'What the Thunder Said', hence his 'OK from here on I think'. It was of this that Eliot later wrote 'A piece of writing meditated, apparently without progress for months and years, may suddenly take shape and word; and in this state long passages may be produced which require little or no retouch'.[26] So it has remained.

e.e.cummings might well be thought to have taken the typewriter as the natural medium for his all but 'shift'less verse, which, with its difficult lineation, was given a very faithful translation into type in *The Dial* in 1923. However, the manuscript shows not just that he wrote with his own hand, but that, while he wrote with type in his mind's eye (hence the unjoined-up script), it was unequal to some of the effects he felt.[27] Some of the 'i's have dots, some not; whatever difference (hard and soft?) he intended, he clearly abandoned for print, hence the pencil note to the compositor in line 3. The four capitals are as clearly marked, but the diaeresis on 'möon' has gone, and so, more surprisingly, has the clearly marked switch to italic in the fourth stanza.

It is difficult to know what Vachel Lindsay may have intended in print when he wrote 'General William Booth Enters into Heaven': it was not type, but the Salvation Army band accompaniment that dominated his imagination.[28] Reproduction cannot easily convey the difference between the first draft in lighter ink, when only a bass drum beats time to the march, on the left. Later, he went over the draft in pencil and darker ink, adding to and correcting the words, scoring in banjos and flutes on the right. In whatever form this reached the compositor in 1913 (typescript?), the press was unequal to vertical as well as horizontal reading, and Lindsay or the printer settled for simple stage-directions.

Mallarmé's *Un coup de dés n'abolira pas le hasard* takes the problem that has haunted poets and their audiences over four thousand years to a logical conclusion: that is, how the evanescent, iridescent idea in the poet's mind is to be registered in graphic form – what, in short, is the *art* of poetry? Others, less perceptive than Claudel, have doubted both conclusion and logic: final or not, *Un coup de dés* has stimulated more criticism and exegesis than almost any other poem. At one level the narrative of a shipwreck, at another the wreck of poetry itself; seen one way, a graphic image of the shipwreck, seen again, a cunningly constructed commentary on itself – all this needs far more time and space than we have here. But note how it changes from the first, to Mallarmé unsatisfactory, appearance in the influential but short-lived Anglo-French journal *Cosmopolis* (1897) in Millar & Richard's 'Old Style' and Latin Antique, to the definitive posthumous text (1914), published by Mallarmé's son-in-law and N.R.F., set in ancient Caslon, newly fashionable in France.

Mallarmé has found but one serious imitator, the Australian poet Christopher Brennan. His *Poems* (1913) shows the same fascination with the appearance of type and letters (different here on facing pages), and his 'I don't give a tinker's curse for the public' sets about its theme as did *Un coup de dés*. The manuscript of 'The Pocket Musicopoematographoscope' has suffered, as did its author. But, *ut pictura poesis*,[29] it is a picture as well as a poem: it was not the first such, nor will it be the last. Picture poems go back to antiquity. The 'Axe of Symmachus', part of the Theocritean corpus, and the famous 'Crucifixion' and other pictorial conceits of Rabanus Maurus, were created before printing came to constrain the poet-artist's freedom. Gratien du Pont's 'Exchequier en forme deue' (1534) made a chessboard into a poem, François Othenin made another into a pair of spectacles (1592), and Robert Angot de l'Eponnière a lute.[30] Thomas Watson's *Hecatompathia* (1582) is

Stephene Mallarmé: Un Coup de Dés Jamais N'Abolira Le Hasard (Paris, N.R.F., 1914).

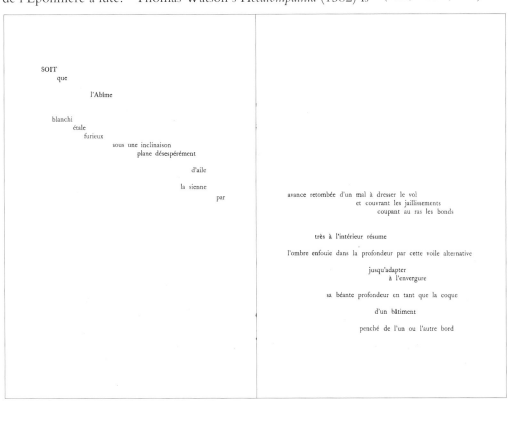

The plumes of night, unfurl'd
and eyed with fire, are whirl'd
slowly above this watch, funereal:
the vast is wide, and yet
no way lies open; set
no bar, but the flat deep rises, a placid wall.

Some throne thou think'st to win
or pride of thy far kin;
this incomplete and dusty hour to achieve:
know that the hour is one,
eternally begun,
eternally deferr'd, thy grasp a Danaid sieve.

O weary realm, O height
the which exhausted flight
familiar finds, home of its prompting ill!
here, there, or there, or there,
ever the same despair;
rest in thy place, O fool, the heart eludes thee still.

Rest—and a new abyss
suddenly yawns, of this
the moment sole, and yet the counterpart:
and thou must house it, thou,
within thy fleshly Now,
thyself the abyss that shrinks, the unbounded hermit-heart:

the mightier heart untold
whose paining depths enfold
all loneliness, all height, all vision'd shores;
and the abyss uncrown'd,
blank failure thro' each bound
from the consummate point thy broken hope implores.

The trees that thro' the tuneful morn had made
bride-dusk for beams that pierce the melting shade,
or thro' the opulent afternoon had stood
lordly, absorb'd in hieratic mood,
now stricken with misgiving of the night
rise black and ominous, as who invite
some fearful coming whose foreblown wind shall bow,
convuls'd and shuddering, each dishevell'd brow:
the garden that had sparkled thro' its sheen
all day, a self-sufficing gem serene,
hiding in emerald depths the vision'd white
of limbs that follow their own clear delight,
exhales towards the inaccessible skies,
commencing, failing, broken, scents or sighs:

Above Christopher Brennan, 'I don't give a tinker's curse', from *Poems* 1913.

Left Urania practica.

Opposite picture poems 'Biedny Poeta'.

the first example of the genre in England, 'My Love is Past' forming 'A Pasquine Piller in despite of Love', while William Browne of Tavistock produced an English 'Cross' poem. George Herbert's *The Temple* enclosed 'The Altar'. Like acrostics, it is easy for such devices to turn into monuments to their own virtuosity, like the paean to the authors of *Urania Practica* (1649), whose couplets form a terrestrial globe. But in Polish hands, a satire on the poor poet calling on a potential publisher, receiving the expected rejection and being kicked downstairs for his pains is given extra edge by its graphic form.

Futurism as such, despite its asserted break with the past, thus responds to a long desire to make poetic words on the tongue or in the mind convey a visible image. How

BIEDNY POETA

Duma na czole, rękopis w kieszeni,
Przekroczył śmiało próg wspaniałej sieni,
Uśmiech na ustach, bo nadzieje duże:

górze.
ku
schodach
po
kroczył
jaką
droga
To

Wydawcę w swym biurze znienacka zaskoczył,
Jął czytać poemat: połowę mu wtłoczył...
Nim skończył czytanie, wyleciał z łomotem:

To droga jaką zjeżdżał po schodach z powrotem!

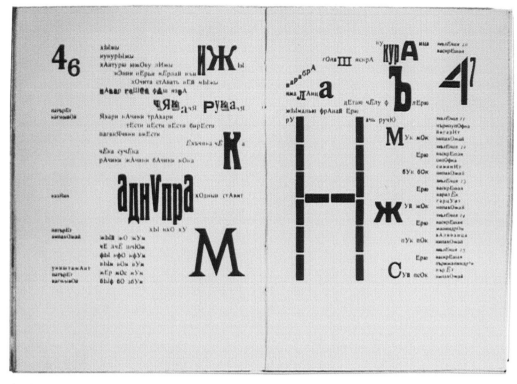

Iliazd *LidantYu Faram.*

far the word and letter pictures of Marinetti should be considered poetry is an open question, one that he would himself left open: that they are poetic is beyond dispute. *Dunes* (1914) and *Zang Tumb Tuuum* (1914) are both visually exciting and convey a poetic message, just as Mayakovsky's *Khorosho!* (1927), Paul van Ostaijen's *Bezette Stad* and Apollinaire's 'Lettre-Océan' (1914) do. There is, in fact, a large distance between these and Apollinaire's *Calligrammes* (1916): by then he had moved on to what is much more an old-fashioned picture poem. The figure that unites them (figuratively) is Iliazd, whose *LidantYu Faram* (1923) is an elegy for his friend Mikhail Ledentu, killed in the First World War. When he came to Paris, this in turn inspired a new French futurism, of which Blaise Cendrars's *Panama ou les Aventures de mes Sept Oncles* is an example. This type of poetic expression was a casualty of the nihilistic explosion of Dadaism, but the apotheosis of the collision between word and image had already come with Cendrars's and Sonia Delaunay's *La prose du Transsibérien et la petite Jehanne* (1913).

'Concrete poetry', a verbal offshoot of Theo van Doesburg's 'Art Concret', goes back to Max Bill, the stormy petrel of post-war typographic innovation, whose contribution to Eugen Gomringer's *33 Konstellationen* ([1945–]1960) gives it a special elegance. The many exponents of concrete poetry, in the 1950s and since, combine (at their best) eye-catching design with verbal wit. Decio Pignatari (*hombre / hambre / hembra* = man / hunger

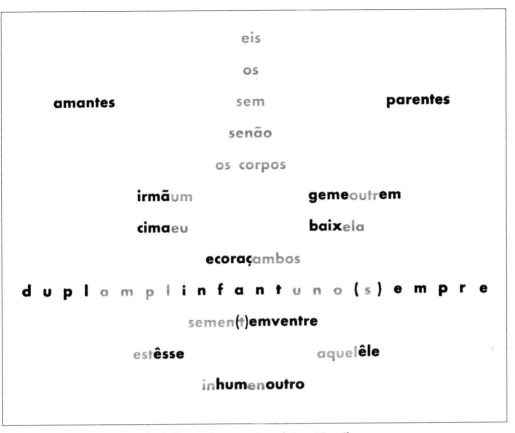

Augusto de Campos,
Noigandres, Rio de Janeiro,
1952.

/ woman), John Furnival (alpha and omega) and Ian Hamilton Finlay ('Au Pair Girl') are mainly verbal; Carlo Belloli ('Acqua'), Emmett Williams ('Like Attracts Like') and Diter Rot (no room, no time) achieve their effects more by the imagery. It is perhaps not surprising that the main impetus in visual poetry of all kinds – the collage-poem, package-poem, montage- or intersign-poem – has come from Brazil, the home of the 'Noigandres' group, where the first International Exhibition of Visual Poetry was held at São Paulo in 1988. Limited by a 'minority' language, Noigandres had an interest in escaping into universal language. 'This introduction of visuality into the sphere of the poetic function disarticulates the divisions among languages, sectioned up and individualized by the ideological system to reflect the conception of the world. This disarticulation is not absolutely intended by the processes of multimedia and interdisciplinarity: these, on the contrary, produce a reinvigoration of the parts, disguising them in an experimental mess where each sign is kept within the limits of its semiotic nature; they share the same space but do not blend or fuse [...] Thus, what determines language (poetic in this case) is not the nature of the sign (if this is verbal, visual, or sound), but the function it exercises.'[31] The result, as in the work Augusto de Campos, is breathtaking.

THE THE THE THE THE BEFORE WE GET TO KNOW EACH OTHER LET ME GIVE YOU THE LOW DOWN GATE

```
        e   r   p
      n           l
     i     A     A    t
     'D    nd    lso  e
       as you I was
       told to walk the
    straight and ⌒ narrow
   to reach my gaol. But
  one bright, grinding and
   sharp bite I found in
    my smother's eyes.
    And I know it's the fas    hion to word stingy CLINK CLINK CLINK CLINK CLINK CLINK
   But to me verbiage don't stink.    I love to roll in words to LINK LINK LINK LINK LINK LINK LINK
  Like the fair IBM used to think it   used to think THINK THINK THINK THINK THINK THINK THINK
 And I ain't afraid to splash in on all  fours in fat Balzac INK INK INK INK INK INK INK INK
 After a generous lifetime of putting u   p with enormous fake moral KINK KINK KINK KINK KINK
 I don't think a chew from choicey   need be so sucked SINK SINK SINK SINK SINK SINK –
 Ok! Ok! So I opened the bright gates,   the everlasting doors. CLINK CLINK CLINK CLINK
 CLINK. So? Is it my fault? Rochester?  Well! Is it my fault at all? ALL ALL ALL ALL
 ALL that stuff that was in there? Gaudi  hot on all that abstrusilated pure golden wall?
 Was miles and miles of laudi, laudi light  encrusted haughty, piles of gaudy smile tiles?         CLINK
 No Popes. No Inmans. No Brahmins. No Lamas. No Rabbis. No. No fake pure angel smiles.          CL
 Can I help it? Is it my fault? Ovidi Nasonis? Paradise is so non-full of non-dolor moral WHORE CLINK.CL NK  CLIN
 Go in back of this white page rack– if you will please CLINK  far enough to go profo  undly back,        I  L C  K
 All there is behind every thing is a great big less than nothing brink drink of absolute n  o light wrack.
 All there is, all you see, friends, pork bellies, amiable non-entities, is bright star wink on  no light black.
 On this poor white sheet brink CLINK  please don't just see a flaming cascade of just plain  good taste gate.
 ☞ !Perhaps the smo  othest assemblage!              Way! Way! down around th e spot that's hot!  ☜
  ☞ !Ever to sing   pleasure's mirth!                    Woo!  !Ever assembl ed here on earth!  ☜
    See a Self al   one on a vacant                      Woo!   rack induldg ing in Self worth–
   And hear one   charming, winged                             non–flying, Porker explain
   Haltingly in the   main hock what                             is in the pen of each refrain.
   Or, like the sweet,  milk large breasts                       of love's best,  our dear Mae West,
   Sense the gates of p  eace, joy, and light     CLINK         delight as your  eyes sink in the rest.
 Stars shine bright on shatter light. In back of that is star CLINK One fat star flat on its CLINK croaks there's no law against screaming
 Refrain right into the end stroke choke. Thee.The.The.That's sooner or later we all come to the burden in the end we must
                                                                                              CLANG, folks,
```

David Daniels, *Years*, Berkeley, 2002.

From this, it is a natural step to electronic or interactive poetry. In material terms this has some very similar attributes. Design is an integral part of the poetic process, but shape can change through the addition of hypertext, animation and multimedia, to which can be added the impossibility of controlling the output, differing with every machine on which it is downloaded. Consequently it is self-reflexive: writers are preoccupied by the medium, annexing material from the internet, its global issues, chat-lines and games. Underlying it is the 'neath text', the programming, which may itself be the poem. It exceeds our present limits to describe, let alone display, this. It is, above all, interactive: it demands reader collaboration, and to be pursued through the Electronic Poetry Center, the Online Writing Centre, and many other sites, corporate and individual. Electronic poets tend to be Mac users, but David Daniels did not despise Microsoft, and the example shown here, downloaded from his website, shows not only great ingenuity but a true poetic gift allied to original diction. The pictograms of 'The Gates of Paradise', a Tennielian gryphon for 'The Before we Get to Know each other, Let me Give You the Low Down Gate', the epic 'The Transformation of Price Krusher

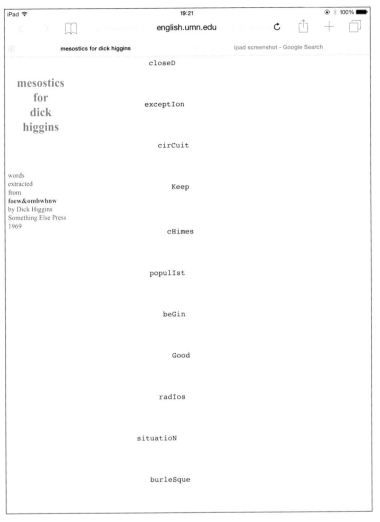

Krapunchki into a Great White Shark Gate' with open jaws are visually as well as verbally telling. I particularly like them.

I conclude with Miekal And's acrostic epitaph for Dick Higgins, whose *Pattern Poetry: Guide to an Unknown Literature* (1987) has been an inspiration to those who explore today the ever widening borderland between picture and poetry. It is, I like to think, full of new and exciting promise…

Envoi?

Poetry, originally an oral means of communication whose purpose was essentially memorial, and transmitted from speech into graphic form, is on the move again. Its original memorial function has long since gone. If poetry was to Wordsworth 'the spontaneous overflow of powerful feelings' that 'takes its origin from emotion recollected in tranquillity',[1] graphic form did more than act as, so to speak, the amanuensis of that emotion. The structures that helped Keats shape and then transcribe those emotions in 'To Autumn' are now indissoluble from the image of poetry, itself the evocation of images. If much modern experiment, from *vers libre* to the kinetic concrete muse, seems an attempt to break the mould that formed that image, the shifting, transient modes of electronic communication offer the possibility of a new image. What that image will be, whether rhyme, stress, metre, script, type or any of the other ancillary devices that have shaped poetic inspiration will survive in new forms, as yet beyond our imagination, remains to be seen.

Notes

Chapter 1: Before the Alphabet

1 See P. Mack, *A History of Renaissance Rhetoric, 1380–1620* (Oxford, 2011).

2 W.P. Ker, *Epic and Romance* (London, 2nd edn, 1908), p. 131.

3 J. Cornet, *Kuba Art and Rule* (Iowa, 2004), p. 15; R. Finnegan, *Oral Literature in Africa* (Cambridge, 2nd edn, 2012), pp. 89–96, 116–20.

4 M. Lichtheim, *Ancient Egyptian Literature* (Berkeley, 1975), vol. I, p. 30.

5 British Museum papyrus, P.10371.

6 BM, EA 10182 = P.Sallier II.1.

7 R.B. Parkinson, *Poetry and Culture in Middle Kingdom Egypt: A Dark Side to Perfection* (New York/Oakville), p. 000.

8 BM, EA 10474.

9 BM, P.Ch.B. IV = EA 10684 'Immortality of Scribes'; R.B. Parkinson, *Voices from Ancient Egypt: An Anthology of Middle Kingdom Writings* (London, 1991), pp. 149–50.

10 *The Library of A. Chester Beatty: Description of a Hieratic Papyrus with a Mythological Story, Love-songs, and Other Miscellaneous Texts*, ed. Alan H. Gardiner (Oxford, 1931), C1, 1–C4, 9; G1, 1–G2, 5.

11 R.B. Parkinson, et al., *Cracking Codes* (Berkeley, 1999), pp. 49–50; J. Bottéro, *Mesopotamia* (Chicago, 1992), pp. 90–94.

12 BM, WAA Sm 954, 'Hymn to Ishtar'. D. MacKenzie, *Myths of Babylonia and Assyria* (London, 1915), pp. 18–20.

13 B. Foster, *Before the Muses: An Anthology of Akkadian Literature* (Bethesda, 1996), I. 71–4.

14 BM, UET 6/2, 414.

15 BM, WA 78941 – Atrahasis 1 & 2.

16 BM, K3375 – Gilgamesh XI 1 & 2.

17 BM, K3972/8396.

18 BM, WA 26187.

19 BM, K 162.

20 BM, K 8204.

21 BM, K 8204 + 34773.

22 Parkinson et al., *Cracking Codes*, pp. 193–94.

Chapter 2. The Alphabet: From East to West

1 M. Fales, *Prima dell' Alfabeto* (Venice, 1989), pp. 175–89.

2 J. Černý, 'Language and Writing', in J.R. Harris (ed.), *The Legacy of Egypt* (Oxford, 2nd edn, 1971), pp. 213–17.

3 D. Diringer, *The Alphabet* (London, 2nd edn, 1949), pp. 199–202, 208–16.

4 In *De Sacra Poesi Hebraeorum* (1753); see J. Kugel, *The Idea of Biblical Poetry* (New Haven, 1981), pp. 12ff.

5 P. Naqlun inv. 67/89; see T. Derda, 'Polish Excavations at Deir el-Naqlun', *Proceedings of the 20th International Congress of Papyrologists, 23–9 August 1992*, ed. A. Bülow-Jacobsen (Copenhagen, Museum Tusculum Press, 1994), 126

6 On Latin *praelectio*, M. Parkes, *Pause and Effect: Punctuation in the West* (Aldershot and Berkeley, 1993), p. 12, p. 117 n. 38, quoting B. Townend, 'Some problems of punctuation in the Latin hexameter', *CQ* 14 (1969), pp. 330ff.

7 Archilochus, H.J. Milne, *Catalogue of the Literary Papyri in the British Museum* (London, 1927), pl. IVa.

8 Euripides, *Hippolytus*, Milne, *Literary Papyri*, pl. IVb.

9 J. Irigoin, 'Ménandre, Les Sicyoniens', in H.-J. Martin (ed.), *Mise en Page et Mise en Texte du Livre Manuscrit* (Paris, 1990), pp. 31–33.

10 H.D. Betz, *Greek Magical Papyri in Translation* (Chicago, 2nd edn, 1992), pp. lvi–lvii.

11 M. Norsa, *Papiri Greci delle Collezioni Italiane: Scritture Documentarie* (Rome, 1929–46), pl. 5b.

12 Axiopistus, *Epicharmea*, c. 300 BC, Grenfell-Hunt, *Hibeh Papyri* I (1906), no. 1, 13.

13 W. Schubart, *Papyri Graeci Berolinenses* (Bonn, 1911), pl. 11b.

14 Schubart, *Papyri Graeci Berolinenses*, pl. 19a.

15 Schubart, *Papyri Graeci Berolinenses*, pl. 19c.

16 E. Maunde Thompson, *Introduction to Greek and Latin Palaeography* (Oxford, 1912), pp. 140–41.

17 BL, P.742.

18 BL, P.733.

19 Cf. Irigoin, 'Ménandre: Les Sicyoniens'. This sort of approach is well illustrated in a fragment of Corinna on the strife of Helicon with Cithaeron, written in a normal second-century hand (Schubart, *Papyri Graeci Berolinenses*, pl. 29a). The text has been set out lineated, with the *paragraphos*, accented, with quantities marked, to which the scholarly writer has added small marginal notes

translating Boeotian dialect words into ordinary (by now Attic) Greek.

20 Galen, *De Placitis Hippocratis et Platonis*, VIII.1.

21 BL, P114.

22 Bodleian, MS Gr.class.c 76/2.

23 Measurement for commercial purposes is a persistent factor in the layout of texts, surviving in the printers' practice of 'casting off' copy.

24 W. Schubart, *Das Buch bei den Griechen und Römern* (Berlin, 2nd edn, 1921), pp. 24ff.

25 Schubart, *Papyri Graeci Berolinenses* (1911), pl. xvii; D.L. Page, *Greek Literary Papyri*, I (London and Cambridge, 1942), pp. 470–75.

26 H.I. Bell, reviewing W.E. Crum, *A Greek–Coptic Glossary*, in *Aegyptus* (1925), pp. 177ff.

27 E. Diehl, *Inscriptiones Latinae* (Bonn, 1912), 6, and A. and J. Gordon, *Album of Dated Latin Inscriptions* (Berkeley, 1958), pl. 81.

28 Gordon and Gordon, *Album*, pl. 10.

29 Parkes, *Pause and Effect*, p. 10.

30 *Journal of Roman Studies* LXIX (1979), 125-5, pl.

31 *Codices Latini Antiquiores: A Palaeographical Guide to Manuscripts prior to the Ninth Century* (Oxford, 1934–72) [CLA], IX.1377.

32 Bibliotheca Apostolica Vaticana [BAV], MS. lat 3226; CLA, I.12.

33 CLA, II.★207.

34 S. Morison, *Politics and Script* (Oxford, 1972), p. 28.

35 Four leaves are in the Vatican Library (BAV, lat. 3256) and three at Berlin (Staatsbibliothek, Cod. lat. fol. 416).

36 Twelve leaves survive in a later assemblage of early texts at St Gallen, MS 1394, CLA, VII.977.

37 The Palatinus, BAV, Pal. 1631, and Romanus, BAV, lat. 3867.

38 St Augustine, *Confessiones*, VI.3.

39 CLA, VI.772.

40 Cambridge, University Library, MS. Ff. 5. 27.

41 E.A. Lowe, *English Uncial* (Oxford, 1960), XIV, XVIII (d), XXXII, XXXIV.

42 On singing and pointing for liturgical chant, cf. Parkes, *Pause and Effect*, p. 129 n. 13, also p. 147 n. 5.

43 S.J.P. Van Dijck, 'Medieval terminology and methods of psalm singing', *Musica Disciplina* VI (1952), pp. 7–26.

44 But evidence of the opposite direction is rare; cf. *Corpus Inscriptionum Latinarum*, X.7296, and Morison, *Politics and Script*, 38.

45 Compare Gordon and Gordon, *Album*, pl. 106.

46 BAV. lat., CLA, I.30, and Milan, Bibliotheca Ambrosiana, Cimelio 2, CLA, III.305.

47 E.A. Lowe, *Palaeographical Papers, 1907–1965* (Oxford, 1972), vol. I, pp. 196–99, 266–68.

48 C. Nordenfalk in *Der Dagulf-Psalter* (Graz, 1980).

49 Österreichische Nationalbibliothek, MS. lat. 1861, f. 4v.

50 BL, Cotton MS. Vespasian B.VI, f. 104; S. Keynes, 'Between Bede and the *Chronicle*: London, BL, Cotton Vespasian B. VI, ff 104–9', in K. O'Brien O'Keefe and A. Orchard (eds.), *Latin Learning and English Lore: Studies for Michael Lapidge* (Toronto, 2005), vol. I, pp. 47–67.

51 Corpus Christi College Cambridge, MS. 223, John the Scot, *Aulae Sidereae*.

52 Parkes, *Pause and Effect*, pp. 12, 27, 97 n. 5, 125 nn. 73, 76, 147 n. 5.

53 M. Parkes, *Scribes, Scripts and Readers* (London, 1991), pp. 259–62.

54 BN, MS. lat. 7926.

55 Ker, *Epic and Romance*, p. 100.

Chapter 3. And Back Again: Latin and Vernacular

1 Parkinson, *Cracking Codes*, p. 103, fig. 39.

2 J. Mallon, *Paléographie romaine* (Scripturae Monumenta et Studia III, Madrid, 1952), pp. 55–73, 89ff; F. Musika, *Krasné Pismo ve výoji Latinki* (Prague, 1958), vol. I, p. 148, fig. 98 and pl. xxii.

3 Parkes, *Pause and Effect*, p. 175.

4 Morison, *Politics and Script*, p. 152.

5 Milan, Biblioteca Ambrosiana, MS. C.5 inf., f. 13v. *Oxford Book of Medieval Latin Verse*, no. 28.

6 Milan, Ambrosiana, MS. C.105, f. 121v (Steffens, 27d), St Gall, 1399.a.1, Isidore, *Etymologies*, Irish s.VII.

7 E. Casamassima, 'Litterae Gothicae: Note per la Storia della Riforma Grafica Umanistica', *La Bibliofilia* LXII (1960), pp. 109–43.

8 CLA, V.587, XI.1629.

9 Parkes, *Pause and Effect*, p. 23.

10 A. Petrucci, 'L'Onciale Romana', *Studi Medievali* XII (1972), pp. 75–131; on contacts between Britain and Spain, see B. Bischoff, *Settimane di Studio* XXII (Spoleto, 1975), p. 299, quoted by Parkes, *Pause and Effect*, p. 125 n. 61.

11 Florence, Biblioteca Medicea-Laurenziana, MS. 39.1, f. 349v.

12 Leiden, Universiteitsbibliotheek, MS.67.

13 Epistola 63, *Monumenta Germaniae Historiae, Epistolae Selectae*, ed. M. Tangl, vol. I (Berlin, 1916), p. 131.

14 M. Lapidge, 'The Study of Greek at the School of Canterbury in the Seventh Century', in M. Herren, *The Sacred Nectar of the Greeks* (London, 1988), pp. 169–94; and in *Anglo-Latin Literature 600–899* (London, 1996). M.R. Godden, 'Literacy in

Anglo-Saxon England', in *The Cambridge History of the Book in Britain*, vol. I (Cambridge, 2012), p. 580.

15 P. Lucas, 'MS Junius 11 and Malmesbury', *Scriptorium* 34 (1980), pp. 197–220; D. Scragg, 'Old English Homiliaries and Poetic Manuscripts', in *The Cambridge History of the Book in Britain*, vol. I (Cambridge, 2012), pp. 556–57.

16 A full list of other manuscripts in M. Gretsch and H. Gneuss, 'Anglo-Saxon Glosses to a Theodorean Poem', in K. O'Brien O'Keefe and A. Orchard (eds.), *Latin Learning and English Lore: Studies for Michael Lapidge* (Toronto, 2005), vol. I, pp. 9–46.

17 Österreichische Nationalbibliothek, MS. 751.

18 *Ibid.*, 321.

19 Bangor Antiphonary, f. 10.

20 Vercelli, Biblioteca Capitolare, MS. XVII.

21 Oxford, Bodleian Library, MS. Junius 11.

22 BN, Lat. 8084.

23 St Petersburg, Q.V. XIX.1.

24 BL, MS. Cotton Vespasian D.XII, f. 83v.

25 Cambridge University Library, MS. Gg.5.35 ('Cambridge Songs'). The Regular Sequence is set out in Victorine stanzas in Bodleian Library, MS. Digby 19, f. 74.

26 Bodley, MS. Lat. misc. d.15, f. 10v.

27 BL, MSS. Cotton Cleopatra A.VIII, Add. 16895 and 22867.

28 BL, MSS. Arundel 384, f. 233, and Burney 305, f. 36. *Oxford Book of Medieval Latin Verse*, pp. 229–32, [233], 238; C.S. Lewis, *The Allegory of Love* (Oxford, 1936), p. 110.

29 Kassel, Murhardsche Bibliothek, MS. theol. 2°. 54 + Bayerische Staatsbibliothek, Clm 2053, 65v–66.

30 Valenciennes, Bibliothèque Municipale, MS.150.

31 Clermont-Ferrand, Bibliothèque Municipale, MS.189/240.

32 Ascoli Piceno, Biblioteca Comunale, MS. XXV. 51; E. Monaci, *Facsimili di Documenti per la Storia delle Lingue e delle Letterature Romanze* (Rome, 1910), no. 61.

33 BN, lat. 3576. Monaci, *Facsimili di Documenti*, no. 47; G. Petraglione, 'Il *Romance de Lope de Moros*', *Studi di Filologia Romanza* 8 (1901), pp. 485–502.

34 Florence, Biblioteca Medicea-Laurenziana, MS. Santa Croce XV.6. E. Monaci, *Facsimile di Antichi Manoscritti per Uso delle Scuole di Filologia Neolatina* (Rome, 1882–91), no. 66.

35 G. Hasenohr, 'Les origines monastiques', in H.-J. Martin (ed.), *Mise en Page et Mise en Texte du Livre Manuscrit* (Paris, 1990), pp. 231–34.

36 Oxford, Bodleian, MS. Digby 23 (Roland); Leiden, Universiteitsbibliotheek, MS. Voss. Lat. 8° 60, (Chanson de St Foy).

37 Bodleian, MS. Fr.d.16, f. 10r (Tristan).

38 BL, Add.38662, Guy of Warwick *c*. 1250.

39 BL, Add.15606, f. 57 + Add.16441 (Athis & Porfilias).

40 Martin (ed.), *Mise en Page*, figs. 201–203; BL, Harley 222 and Royal 20.A.III.

41 Bodleian, Junius 1.

42 Facsimiles in G.L. Brook and R.F. Leslie, *Layamon's Brut*, EETS, O.S. 250 (1963) and 277 (1978); Parkes, *Pause and Effect*, p. 104.

43 BL, Cotton MS. Caligula A.ix + Jesus 29.

44 Cambridge University Library MS. Kk iv.24.

45 BL, Harley 2253.

46 Cambridge, University Library, MS. Add.4122.

47 BL, Cotton Nero A.x.

48 BL, Add.32578.

49 BL, Cotton Caligula A.II.

50 BL, Arundel 38, f. 39v.

51 Examples of all three are in Bodleian, MS. Digby 181, the Huntington Library's famous 'Ellesmere Chaucer', and BL, Harley 7184.

52 Pierpont Morgan Library, New York M.819 (Chansonnier occitan)

53 BL.Royal 16.F.II, a royal presentation copy, and BN, fr.25458 (the 'chansonnier').

54 Hill's is Balliol College, Oxford, MS.354, while the Bodleian has Fortescue's and Rate's, MSS. Digby 145 and Ashmole 61.

55 G. Hasenohr, 'Vers une nouvelle esthétique', in Martin (ed.), *Mise en Page*, pp. 349–52.

56 Cambridge, University Library, MS. Ff.3.31.

57 N. Barker, '*Grammatica Rhythmica*: Copy, Text and Layout, 1466–1468', *Hellinga Festschrift* (Amsterdam, 1980), pp. 43–57.

Chapter 4. The Poet on the Page

1 M. Porena, *Il Codice Vaticano lat.3196 autografo del Petrarca* (Vatican, 1941); M. Vatasso, *L'Originale del Canzoniere di…Petrarca* (Milan, 1905).

2 British Library, King's 321 (Petrarch), Add. 16564 (Petrarch).

3 BL, Add. 46919 (Herbert) and Add. 16165 (Shirley).

4 A.B. Emden, *A Biographical Register of the University of Oxford to 1500* (Oxford, 1958), and A. Jotischky in *Oxford Dictionary of National Biography.*

5 A.I. Doyle, 'More Light on John Shirley', *Medium Aevum* XXX (1961), pp. 93–101.

6 Lydgate, whose works appeared in many more separate editions throughout the end of the fifteenth and early sixteenth century, disappears abruptly about 1530.

7 *La Naissance du Livre Moderne*, ed. H.-J. Martin (Paris, 2000), figs. 314–18, 283.

8 A. Petrucci, 'Alle origini del libro moderno: libri da banco, libri di bisaccia, libretti da mano', *Italia Medioevale e Umanistica* XII (1969), pp. 295–313.

9 *En français dans le texte* (Paris, 1990), pp. 68–69; *Printing and the Mind of Man, British Museum Section* (London, 1963), no. 71.

10 *Octantetrois Pseaumes* (Geneva, 1543), f. 7.

11 *Discorsi dell'arte poetica e del poema eroico*, ed. L. Poma (Bari, 1964), vol. II, p. 89.

12 T. Tasso, *Le Lettere*, ed. C. Guasti (Florence, 1854–55), vol. II, pp. 257–58.

13 B. del Bene, *Civitas Veri* (Paris, 1609), p. 10; quoted in Martin (ed.), *La Naissance du Livre Moderne*, p. 240.

14 Egerton MS.2711.

15 L. Delisle, *Le Cabinet des Manuscrits de la Bibliothèque Impériale*, I (1868), p. 398.

16 Martin (ed.), *La Naissance du Livre Moderne*, fig. 288.

17 H. Love, *Scribal Publication in Seventeenth-century England* (Oxford, 1993); P. Beal et al., *Index of English Literary Manuscripts* (London, 1980–93); idem, *In Praise of Scribes: Manuscripts and their Makers in 17th-century England* (Oxford, 1999).

18 M. Hobbs, 'Early 17th-century Verse Miscellanies', in *English Manuscript Studies 1100–1700*, I (Oxford, 1989), pp. 182–210.

19 *Index of English Literary Manuscripts*, I. HrJ 9–10.

20 Bodleian, MS. Rawl. poet.125.

21 Add. 18920.

22 *Index of English Literary Manuscripts*, I.125, HrJ 11–16, 243.

23 MS.2062, f. 7.

24 J. Lennard, *But I Digress: The Exploitation of Parentheses in English Printed Verse* (Oxford, 1991), pp. 25–26.

25 Bodleian, MS.Eng. poet. d.197.

26 *Index of English Literary Manuscripts*, I. DoJ 1859–77.

Chapter 5. The Muse in Print

1 Jones B 62.

2 Lennard, *But I Digress*, p. 50.

3 P. Croft, *Autograph Poetry in the English Language* (London, 1973), p. 36, a fair copy sent to Sir Dudley Carleton.

4 Lennard, *But I Digress*, pp. 26–27; for similar use by Sidney and Marvell, see pp. 44, 54.

5 Bodleian, MS. Rawl. poet.88, 77–8.

6 Lennard, *But I Digress*, p. 54. See p. 109.

7 P. Gaskell, *From Writer to Reader: Studies in Editorial Method* (Oxford, 1978), pp. 29–62.

8 BL, Lansdowne MS. 1045, f. 101.

9 Bodleian Library, C. 2. 21 Art.

10 M. England and J. Sparrow, *Hymns Unbidden: Donne, Herbert, Blake, Emily Dickinson and the Hymnographers* (New York, 1966).

11 *Hymns Ancient and Modern*, ed. W.H. Monk (London, 1861).

12 The autograph is in the Biblioteca Nazionale di Napoli, MS. ex Vind. lat. 72; see A. Oldcorn, *The Textual Problems of Tasso's 'Gerusalemme Conquistata'* (Ravenna, 1976).

13 A. Griffiths, *The Print in Stuart Britain, 1603–89* (London, 1998), pp. 184–89.

14 H. Kelliher, *Andrew Marvell, Poet & Politician 1628–78* (London, 1978), pp. 121–24.

15 F.S. Tupper, 'Mary Palmer, alias Mrs Andrew Marvell', *Publications of the Modern Language Association of America*, LIII (1938), pp. 367–92.

16 Bodleian Library, MS. Eng. poet. d. 49.

17 Lennard, *But I Digress*, pp. 58–60.

18 Quoted in Love, *Scribal Publication in Seventeenth-century England*, p. 241.

19 Nottingham University Library, Portland MS. Pw V 31.

20 Bodleian, MS. Eng. Poet. c. 1.

21 *The Correspondence of Alexander Pope*, ed. G. Sherburn (Oxford, 1956), vol. I, p. 214.

22 J. Spence, *Anecdotes, Observations and Characters of Books and Men*, ed. J. Osborn (Oxford, 1966), vol, I, p. 14, no. 30.

23 Written, *teste se ipso* (*Miscellanies*, 1711), in 1706, it was preceded in print by the broadside *Elegy on Pa[r]tridge* (1708).

24 New York, Pierpont Morgan Library, MS. MA 457 [Croft 62], and BL, 11633 e.56.

25 BL, Egerton 2023, [Croft 68] *The Tea-Table Miscellany*, II (Edinburgh, 1726).

26 MSS. Four Oaks, now in the Houghton Library, Harvard.

27 *The Letters of Samuel Johnson*, ed. B. Redford (Princeton, 1992), vol. I, p. 14.

28 *Life* [1766], ed. G. Birkbeck Hill (Oxford, 1888), vol. II, p. 15.

29 J. Bidwell, 'Designs by Mr J. Baskerville for Six Poems by Mr. T. Gray', *The Book Collector*, 51 (2002), pp. 355–71.

30 Manchester, Chetham's Library MS; published as a broadside and in *Harrop's Manchester Mercury*, 19 December 1752, and in Byrom's *Miscellaneous Poems*, 1773.

31 See 'For a' that' MS and *Scots Musical Magazine* II (1788), p. 26.

Chapter 6. The Muse Conscious of Form

1 The distinction of logic and rhetoric in punctuation is Bacon's; see Parkes, *Pause and Effect*, p. 89 and

n. 129, and pp. 110–11, 114.

2 Harvard University, Houghton Library, Keats Collection.

3 *The Letters of John Keats*, ed. Hyder E. Rollins (Cambridge, 1958), II, pp. 208–12.

4 R. Monckton Milnes, *Life, Letters, and Literary Remains, of John Keats* (London, 1848).

5 A.N.L. Munby, *The Cult of the Autograph Letter* (London, 1962), p. 11.

6 BN., MS. nouv.acq.fr.14013, f. 16.

7 Croft, *Autograph Poetry*, p. 113.

8 The latter is not an exclamation mark, a rare error by Croft.

9 Harvard University, Houghton Library, MS. Am 1340 (94–5).

10 Manuscript in the Rosenbach Museum and Library, Philadelphia.

11 *Opere di Giacomo Leopardi: edizione accresciuta, ordianta e corretta secondo l'ultimo intendimento dell' autore* (Florence, 1889).

12 *Opere Scelte* (Torino, U.T.E.T., 1993).

13 Gaskell, *From Writer to Reader*, pp. 118–41.

14 6 September 1862.

15 G.H. Lewes, quoted by E. Griffiths, *The Printed Voice of Victorian Poetry* (Oxford, 1989), p. 61.

16 BL, Add. MS. 43485; *The Ring and the Book*, I (1868), pp. 148–49, 165–68.

17 *The Letters of Oscar Wilde*, ed. R. Hart-Davis (London, 1962), pp. xii–xiii.

18 Manuscript in the William Andrews Clark Memorial Library, Los Angeles.

19 *Letters of Oscar Wilde*, pp. 76–77.

20 BN, Impr.Rés. g.Y.32, f. 22.

21 G. Robb, *Unlocking Mallarmé* (Yale, 1996), p. 213.

22 An earlier, but to Mallarmé unsatisfactory, version of the poem had appeared in the journal *Cosmopolis* in 1897.

23 C. Galantaris, *Verlaine Rimbaud Mallarmé: catalogue raisonné d'une collection* (Paris and Geneva, 2000), p. 392.

24 The manuscript of 'The Master and the Leaves' is in Dorset County Museum.

25 V. Eliot, *The Waste Land: A Facsimile and Transcript of the Original Drafts Including the Annotations of Ezra Pound* (London, 1971).

26 T.S. Eliot, 'The *Pensées* of Pascal', in *Pascal's Pensées*, translated by W.F. Trotter (London, 1931), pp. vii–xix.

27 University of Virginia, Clifton Waller Barrett Library MS. 6246-a; Croft, *Autograph Poetry*, p. 180.

28 Harvard University, Houghton Library, fMS Am 1367; Croft, *Autograph Poetry*, p. 164.

29 Horace, *Ars Poetica*, 361.

30 These examples are from A. Coron, *Avant Apollinaire: Vingt Siècles de Poèmes Figurés* (Marseille, 2005). Coron also reproduces Juan Caramuel Lobkowicz's multiple circular maze poems (*Metametrica*, 1663), a *tour de force* of baroque conceit.

31 Philadelpho Menezes, *Poetics and Visuality: A Trajectory of Contemporary Brazilian Poetry*, trans. H. Polkinghorn (San Diego, 1995), introduction.

Envoi

1 *Lyrical Ballads*, preface.

.

Select Bibliography

Barker, N., '*Grammatica Rhythmica*: Copy, Text and Layout, 1466–1468', *Hellinga Festschrift* (Amsterdam, 1980), pp. 43–57.

Beal, P., et al., *In Praise of Scribes: Manuscripts and their Makers in 17th-century England* (Oxford, 1999).

—*Index of English Literary Manuscripts* (London, 1980–93).

Betz, H. D., *Greek Magical Papyri in Translation* (Chicago, 2nd edn, 1992).

Bidwell, J., 'Designs by Mr J. Baskerville for Six Poems by Mr. T. Gray', *The Book Collector*, 51 (2002), pp. 355–71.

Bottéro, J., *Mesopotamia* (Chicago, 1992).

Burke, C, *Printing Poetry: a Workbook in Typographic Reification* (San Francisco, 1980).

Casamassima, E., 'Litterae Gothicae: Note per la Storia della Riforma Grafica Umanistica', *La Bibliofilia* LXII (1960), pp. 109–43.

Černý, J., 'Language and Writing', in J. R. Harris (ed.), *The Legacy of Egypt* (Oxford, 2nd edn, 1971).

Codices Latini Antiquiores: A Palaeographical Guide to Manuscripts prior to the Ninth Century (Oxford, 1934–72).

Cornet, J., *Kuba Art and Rule* (Iowa, 2004).

Coron, A., *Avant Apollinaire: Vingt Siècles de Poèmes Figurés* (Marseille, 2005).

Croft, P., *Autograph Poetry in the English Language* (London, 1973).

Delisle, L., *Le Cabinet des Manuscrits de la Bibliothèque Impériale*, I (1868).

Diehl, E., *Inscriptiones Latinae* (Bonn, 1912).

Diringer, D., *The Alphabet* (London, 2nd edn, 1949).

Doyle, A. I., 'More Light on John Shirley', *Medium Aevum* XXX (1961), pp. 93–101.

Eliot, T. S., 'The *Pensées* of Pascal', in *Pascal's Pensées*, translated by W. F. Trotter (London, 1931), pp. vii–xix.

Eliot, V., *The Waste Land: A Facsimile and Transcript of the Original Drafts Including the Annotations of Ezra Pound* (London, 1971).

Emden, A. B., *A Biographical Register of the University of Oxford to 1500* (Oxford, 1958).

En francais dans le texte (Paris, 1990).

England, M., and J. Sparrow, *Hymns Unbidden: Donne, Herbert, Blake, Emily Dickinson and the Hymnographers* (New York, 1966).

Fales, M., *Prima dell' Alfabeto* (Venice, 1989).

Finnegan, R., *Oral Literature in Africa* (Cambridge, 2nd edn, 2012).

Foster, B., *Before the Muses: An Anthology of Akkadian Literature* (Bethesda, 1996).

Galantaris, C., *Verlaine Rimbaud Mallarmé: catalogue raisonné d'une collection* (Paris and Geneva, 2000).

Gardiner, Alan H. (ed.), *The Library of A. Chester Beatty: Description of a Hieratic Papyrus with a Mythological Story, Love-songs, and Other Miscellaneous Texts* (Oxford, 1931).

Gaskell, P., *From Writer to Reader: Studies in Editorial Method* (Oxford, 1978).

Godden, M. R., 'Literacy in Anglo-Saxon England', in *The Cambridge History of the Book in Britain*, vol. I (Cambridge, 2012), p. 580.

Gordon, A. and J., *Album of Dated Latin Inscriptions* (Berkeley, 1958).

Gretsch, M., and H. Gneuss, 'Anglo-Saxon Glosses to a Theodorean Poem', in K. O'Brien O'Keefe and A. Orchard (eds.), *Latin Learning and English Lore: Studies for Michael Lapidge* (Toronto, 2005), vol. I, pp. 9–46.

Griffiths, A., *The Print in Stuart Britain, 1603–89* (London, 1998).

Griffiths, E., *The Printed Voice of Victorian Poetry* (Oxford, 1989).

Hart-Davis, R. (ed.), *The Letters of Oscar Wilde* (London, 1962).

Hasenohr, G., 'Les origines monastiques', in H.-J. Martin (ed.), *Mise en Page et Mise en Texte du Livre Manuscrit* (Paris, 1990).

Hobbs, M., 'Early 17th-century Verse Miscellanies', in *English Manuscript Studies*

1100–1700, I (Oxford, 1989), pp. 182–210.

Irigoin, J., 'Ménandre, Les Sicyoniens', in H.-J. Martin (ed.), *Mise en Page et Mise en Texte du Livre Manuscrit* (Paris, 1990).

Kelliher, H., *Andrew Marvell, Poet & Politician 1628–78* (London, 1978).

Ker, W. P., *Epic and Romance* (London, 2nd edn, 1908).

Keynes, S., 'Between Bede and the *Chronicle*: London, BL, Cotton Vespasian B. VI, ff 104-9', in K. O'Brien O'Keefe and A. Orchard (eds.), *Latin Learning and English Lore: Studies for Michael Lapidge* (Toronto, 2005), vol. I, pp. 47–67.

Kugel, J., *The Idea of Biblical Poetry* (New Haven, 1981).

Lapidge, M., 'The Study of Greek at the School of Canterbury in the Seventh Century', in M. Herren, *The Sacred Nectar of the Greeks* (London, 1988), pp. 169–94.

Lennard, J., *But I Digress: The Exploitation of Parentheses in English Printed Verse* (Oxford, 1991).

Leopardi, G., *Opere di Giacomo Leopardi: edizione accresciuta, ordianta e corretta secondo l'ultimo intendimento dell' autore* (Florence, 1889).

Lewis, C. S., *The Allegory of Love* (Oxford, 1936).

Lichtheim, M., *Ancient Egyptian Literature* (Berkeley, 1975).

Love, H., *Scribal Publication in Seventeenth-century England* (Oxford, 1993).

Lowe, E. A., *English Uncial* (Oxford, 1960).

—*Palaeographical Papers, 1907–1965* (Oxford, 1972).

Mack, P. *A History of Renaissance Rhetoric, 1380–1620* (Oxford, 2011).

MacKenzie, D., *Myths of Babylonia and Assyria* (London, 1915).

Mallon, J., *Paléographie romaine* (Scripturae Monumenta et Studia III, Madrid, 1952).

Martin, H.-J. (ed.), *La Naissance du Livre Moderne* (Paris, 2000).

Maunde Thompson, E., *Introduction to Greek and Latin Palaeography* (Oxford, 1912).

Menezes, P., *Poetics and Visuality: A Trajectory of Contemporary Brazilian Poetry*, trans. H. Polkinghorn (San Diego, 1995).

Monaci, E., *Facsimile di Antichi Manoscritti per Uso delle Scuole di Filologia Neolatina* (Rome, 1882–91).

—*Facsimili di Documenti per la Storia delle Lingue e delle Letterature Romanze* (Rome, 1910).

Monckton Milnes, R., *Life, Letters, and Literary Remains, of John Keats* (London, 1848).

Monk, W. H. (ed.), *Hymns Ancient and Modern* (London, 1861).

Morison, S., *Politics and Script* (Oxford, 1972).

Munby, A. N. L., *The Cult of the Autograph Letter* (London, 1962).

Norsa, M., *Papiri Greci delle Collezioni Italiane: Scritture Documentarie* (Rome, 1929–46).

Oldcorn, A., *The Textual Problems of Tasso's 'Gerusalemme Conquistata'* (Ravenna, 1976).

Page, D. L., *Greek Literary Papyri*, I (London and Cambridge, 1942).

Parkes, M., *Pause and Effect: Punctuation in the West* (Aldershot and Berkeley, 1993).

—*Scribes, Scripts and Readers* (London, 1991).

Parkinson, R. B., *Reading Ancient Egyptian Poetry: Among Other Histories* (Chichester/ Malden, 2009).

—*Voices from Ancient Egypt: An Anthology of Middle Kingdom Writings* (London, 1991).

—, et al., *Cracking Codes* (Berkeley, 1999).

Petraglione, G., 'Il *Romance de Lope de Moros*', *Studi de Filologia Romanza* 8 (1901), pp. 485–202.

Petrucci, A., 'Alle origini del libro moderno: libri da banco, libri di bisaccia, libretti da mano', *Italia Medioevale e Umanistica* XII (1969), pp. 295–313.

—'L'Onciale Romana', *Studi Medievali* XII (1972), pp. 75–131.

Poma, L. (ed.), *Discorsi dell'arte poetica e del poema eroico* (Bari, 1964).

Porena, M., *Il Codice Vaticano lat.3196 autografo del Petrarca* (Vatican, 1941).

Printing and the Mind of Man, British Museum Section (London, 1963).

Redford, B. (ed.), *The Letters of Samuel Johnson* (Princeton, 1992).

Robb, G., *Unlocking Mallarmé* (Yale, 1996).

Rollins, H. E. (ed.), *The Letters of John Keats* (Cambridge, 1958).

Sanders, J. A., *Discoveries in the Judaean Desert. 4. The Psalms Scroll of Qumrân, Cave 11* (Oxford, 1965).

Schubart, W., *Das Buch bei den Griechen und Römern* (Berlin, 2nd edn, 1921).